A RABBI LOOKS

AT THE

LAST DAYS

Surprising Insights on Israel,
the End Times and Popular Misconceptions

JONATHAN BERNIS

Chosen

a division of Baker Publishing Group
Minneapolis, Minnesota

Published by Chosen Books
11400 Hampshire Avenue South
Bloomington, Minnesota 55438
www.chosenbooks.com

Chosen Books is a division of
Baker Publishing Group, Grand Rapids, Michigan

Printed in the United States of America

Library of Congress Cataloging-in-Publication Data

Bernis, Jonathan.
    A rabbi looks at the last days : surprising insights on Israel, the end times, and popular misconceptions / Jonathan Bernis.
        p. cm.
    Summary: "Respected messianic rabbi and television host Jonathan Bernis reveals surprising insights about popular misconceptions, Israel, the end times, and a clear sign Christians are ignoring"—Provided by publisher.
    Includes bibliographical references (p.   ).
    ISBN 978-0-8007-9569-6 (cloth : alk. paper)
    ISBN 978-0-8007-9543-6 (pbk. : alk. paper)
    1. End of the world. 2. Bible—Prophecies—Israel. 3. Jewish Christians. 4. Messianic Judaism. I. Title.
BT877.B47 2013
236′.9—dc23   2012034619

In keeping with biblical principles of creation stewardship, Baker Publishing Group advocates the responsible use of our natural resources. As a member of the Green Press Initiative, our company uses recycled paper when possible. The text paper of this book is composed in part of post-consumer waste.

Cover design by Dan Pitts

13 14 15 16 17 18 19   7 6 5 4 3 2 1

green
press
INITIATIVE

Over thirty years ago, when I was a university student studying business, a friend named Suzie made it her project to lead me to the Lord. She brought me to a Bible study where I was confronted with the Gospel and eventually prayed a prayer. I don't even remember the exact words of that prayer, but my life has never been the same since. Thank you, Suzie, for your faithfulness and perseverance. And thank you, Ernie and Maria Beck, for leading that wonderful Bible study for so many years!

Contents

Contents

Preface

A great event is taking place in the world, and almost nobody seems to notice.

It amazes me that many Christian authors who are focused on the last days do not seem to be aware of what is happening in the Jewish community around the world.

Just as the Bible predicted, the Jewish people are being restored to their land and to their Messiah. Not in some far distant end times—but right now!

Although Jewish people who accept *Yeshua HaMashiach* (Jesus the Messiah) are often ostracized by their families, friends and business associates, Jews all over the world are turning to Him and becoming Messianic Jews in numbers not seen since the first century.

I am weary of reading the dogmatic positions expressed in much apocalyptic literature. Some authors will tell you with absolute confidence that they know exactly when and where the significant events of eschatology are to take place. Yet in most instances they ignore some of the clearest prophetic promises concerning the last days.

Perhaps the saddest reality of all is that predominant eschatological positions today frequently impede efforts by evangelical believers to reach Jewish people with the Gospel—and discount the relevance of doing so.

I have written this book in juxtaposition with what is out there on the subject of the last days. Like the little mirror on the right side of your car suggests, "Objects in your mirror are closer than you think."

I hope you enjoy reading this book. And if you have any Jewish friends in your life who may be open to reading it, pass it along to them.

Acknowledgments

I am so thankful to the Lord for the incredible people He has, by His grace, brought into my life. They have been my inspiration and a source of great joy.

First, to my beautiful wife, Elisangela, and my two precious daughters, Liel and Hannah. From the moment I leave on one of my many missions trips, I miss you and can't wait to return home. Every day I am gone I dream of that moment when I return and am met at our door with your excited screams, "Papai is home!" I love you more than you can ever imagine!

To the amazing team at Jewish Voice Ministries International, the ministry the Lord has given me the privilege to lead. Your dedication, commitment to excellence and hard work is a source of inspiration daily, and I am so grateful to each and every one of you. Together, we have done great things and will continue to do great things "exceedingly, abundantly, beyond all we can ask or think."

To Mary Ellen Breitwiser, Grace Sarber and Jane Campbell for driving this project and me to the finish line. I could not have done it without you!

To the tens of thousands of Jewish Voice supporters and friends. Your partnership in the Gospel has enabled us to go to some of the most remote places on earth to help Jewish communities in need and provide them with free medical care and the Gospel. We could not do what we do without you.

And finally (and most importantly), to my beloved Yeshua HaMashiach. *Thank You for redeeming my life.*

PART ONE

"...AND THEN THE END WILL COME"

1

What If Everything You Have Been Told about the Last Days Is Wrong?

The mark of the beast . . . Gog and Magog . . . 666 . . . a confederation of ten nations . . . the Antichrist's ascendancy to power . . . the abomination of desolation . . . Bible teachers point to these as signs that the end of the world as we know it is near.

Many Christians have become obsessed with trying to unravel the Bible's mysterious and veiled prophecies about such things. They analyze every word in the daily newspapers and television news shows to see if they can identify a connection to the last days. This is especially true when there is news of Israel or the Middle East. While they focus on such esoteric matters, they do not seem to notice other and far more obvious signs that the last days are upon us.

What if much of what you have been told about the end times is wrong, or at the very least off target? What if you have looked for the signs of Messiah's return in all the wrong places?

Before we go any further, let me explain that there is nothing wrong with seeking to understand Bible prophecy and live in the light of that understanding. This is precisely what God expects us to do. I am not saying, "Stop trying to understand the book of Revelation." But if we focus too much on red heifers or who the Antichrist is, then we will miss out on the marvelous things God is doing right now to prepare the world for the Messiah's return.

About Me

With the title *A Rabbi Looks at the Last Days*, I am sure you expected a book written by a traditional rabbi. That is not the case. I am, in fact, a "Messianic" rabbi. Please allow me to explain.

A Messianic Jew is a Jew by birth who has come to believe that Jesus—we call Him by His Hebrew name, *Yeshua*—is the promised Messiah of Israel. As Jews, we also believe that we, like the first-century believers, who all happened to be Jewish, have a responsibility to retain our Jewish identity.

I was born a Jew and raised by my Jewish parents in a traditional Jewish home in Rochester, New York. I was a "holiday Jew." We went to synagogue for the High Holidays and celebrated the other significant Jewish feasts such as Passover, Sukkot and Chanakkuh.

Throughout my childhood I attended religious classes at the synagogue on Sundays and Hebrew school on Tuesday and Thursday afternoons in preparation for my bar mitzvah (Jewish rite of passage for males) at age thirteen.

I was well versed about God's divine intervention in our ancient past, including the call of Abraham, the ten plagues and the deliverance of the children of Israel out of Egypt, the parting of the Red Sea, the conquest of Joshua, Daniel in the lions' den, Samson and his supernatural strength tied to his long hair and other stories of renown. I always believed in God but felt my spiritual "duty" had been fulfilled by making it through my bar mitzvah. Still, I knew that my Jewish identity was somehow important.

As a high school athlete (of marginal ability), my first real exposure to the Gospel came through one of my wrestling coaches. This All-American athlete who was also a "born-again Christian" impressed me. It intrigued me to hear him talk about his faith in such a personal way. Until this experience, I thought of Jesus simply as the "son of Mr. and Mrs. Christ," the one who had somehow become the God of another religion called Christianity. At my coach's invitation, I went on a youth trip to Florida with a group called Young Life and attended their meetings for about a year. I enjoyed the fun and even the messages I heard from the New Testament but kept at arm's length the well-meaning believers who shared with me. Jesus was simply not an option for me. I was Jewish, and it was made clear to me as a child that Jews do not believe in Jesus. I was born a Jew and would die a Jew.

A Holy Change in Plans

I knew I had a head for business (which I had inherited from my grandfather on my mother's side), and I had one goal: to be a rich and successful businessman by age thirty. After graduating from high school in my hometown of Rochester, New York, I went off to university in the neighboring city of Buffalo to earn a degree in business and start making as much money as possible as quickly as possible. God, however, had other ideas.

At college I began experimenting with drugs, Eastern meditation and the occult. "Mind-expanding" drugs and the supernatural realm became major pursuits and occupied my free time. But all this changed radically when a friend with whom I used to do drugs got saved.

She had become consumed with drugs. She quit going to class. She stopped eating. I could not watch her continue to destroy herself, so eventually I lost contact with her.

You can imagine how shocked I was when I ran into her one day and she looked completely well and healthy. Light sparkled in her eyes. When she saw me, the happy grin on her face grew even bigger. Everything about her was different.

"I Have Been Born Again!"

Before I could think better of it, I blurted out, "What in the world happened to you?" I realize now how rude that sounds, but I really could not help myself. It was as if she had come back from the walking dead.

"I've been born again!" she said.

"You've been what?" I asked.

"Born again," she laughed. "I've made Jesus Christ the Lord of my life."

Oh no, I thought. *What have I gotten myself into?* But before I could get away, she proceeded with great enthusiasm to tell me that she had turned to Jesus, and that He had set her free from her addiction. The desire had just gone away. One instant, she was a hopeless addict. The next, the craving had vanished.

I could not deny the evidence standing right in front of me, but I did not want to accept what she was telling me. I thought, *If it worked for you, fine, but I have other plans for my life.* I just wanted to get away from her, and that took at least ten minutes.

Even then, I could not get away. For the next few weeks she called me every day, asking questions such as, "Do you know why you're here on earth?" and "If you died right now, where would you go?"

At first I politely tried to brush her off, but I was beginning to sense a certain pressure. Her questions haunted me. Why *was* I here? Where *would* I go if I died? Her words had impact because there was no denying that something amazing and real had happened to her. She was not the same person I had known before.

No Place for a Jewish Boy

After numerous invitations, I finally agreed to go with her to a home Bible study she had been attending. From the moment I walked into the room, I wanted to turn around and run. Clearly this was no place for a good Jewish boy to be—especially one who was still using drugs.

But I could not leave. My only mode of transportation was a motorcycle, and it was a terribly stormy night. I was soaked to the skin by the time I arrived. The wife of the Bible study leader gave me some dry clothes to wear while my clothes tumbled around in her dryer throughout the evening. I could not leave without my clothes!

The study seemed to go on for hours, although it was probably only ninety minutes or so. I was miserable. Everyone seemed to be staring at me. I felt completely out of place and knew everyone sensed my extreme discomfort.

In addition, the leader of the study was originally from Germany and still had a decidedly German accent. This made me uncomfortable as well. After all, I had been brought up believing that the world was divided into two groups: Jews and Christians/Gentiles. And I believed that Christians, especially German ones, hated us. Because of the horrors of the Holocaust, I had a subconscious fear of all Germans, and this encounter triggered this discomfort.

After the study, he invited me to meet with him privately upstairs. Although I was uncomfortable, upstairs meant closer to the front door and my escape, so I followed him to the living room and sat down on the couch, where we were joined by an older gentleman. He placed a Bible on my lap and began to lead me through various Bible verses. He began with Romans 3:23, "For all have sinned and fall short of the glory of God." *Interesting.* I knew I was a sinner, because of my wild college lifestyle, but it was the first time in my life that I was aware of my physical separation from God. Then he took me to Romans 6:23, which said, "For the wages of sin is death, but the gift of God is eternal life in Christ [Messiah] Jesus our Lord."

At that moment I had what I can only describe as a supernatural experience. Although I did not have a vision or hear a heavenly voice, I do not know what else to call it. The room became abnormally bright and warm. I began to sweat profusely, and I can honestly say that I felt as though that couch had arms that reached out and grabbed me—holding me in place. My experience was so significant that I wondered if perhaps the room had been rigged in such a way as to produce this amazing response! I even went back later to inspect that couch and the lighting in the room but found nothing irregular about either one.

That night I began to deal with a sense of my own separation from a God who loved me, Jonathan Bernis, a twenty-year-old college student. At the same time, I struggled with an innate understanding that this direction meant abandoning my own goals and ambitions. Looking back, I am convinced that the presence of God came into the room that evening and apprehended me. God had a plan for my life that was different from my own, and He meant to make sure I would lay aside my plans and follow Him.

Over the next few days, I developed a tremendous hunger to read the Bible, but I did not have one and did not know where to get one. I now wanted to read the New Testament in particular, but where does a good Jewish boy go to shop for a New Testament? I could not go to my friends—they were all drug users. I could not go to the rabbi—he surely would not have one. I had no idea that the Bible was the bestselling book of all time, and I could have bought one at any grocery store or even pharmacy!

Finally I remembered that the high school wrestling coach I mentioned earlier had given me a Bible and said I would need it someday. I had thrown it into a box in my closet at home and forgotten about it.

I jumped on my motorcycle, drove more than sixty miles to my parents' house, ran up to my room and dug through the box in the closet until I found the Bible. I ran back out of the house without ever saying hello or good-bye to my parents and drove back to my dorm room, where I devoured the Scriptures. I could not get enough.

I do not know what I expected to find in the New Testament. I had been taught it was a book for Christians and that it had no connection whatsoever to me as a Jew or to anything I learned in synagogue growing up.

You can imagine my shock when I first opened the book of Matthew and immediately found references to Abraham, Isaac, David and the other Jewish heroes I had learned about as a child. I could not understand, however, what these great figures of Judaism were doing in the Christian Bible. *Was there a parallel universe? Were there two Abrahams—a Christian Abraham and a Jewish Abraham, the father of the Jewish people? Was there a Christian David and a Jewish David? What about the other Jewish heroes? Was there a Jewish Isaac and a Christian parallel? Had they converted to Christianity and no one had ever told me?*

My mind was reeling! As I continued to read over the next few days and weeks, I discovered that Jesus was not the God of the Gentiles, as I had been told, but was in fact Yeshua, the Messiah of Israel. I was stunned as I learned that Yeshua was born to Jewish parents in the Jewish homeland of Israel, and that all His first followers were Jews.

Then I searched through the Hebrew Scriptures, my own Torah, prophets and writings (the Tanakh or Old Testament), and was even more shocked to find literally hundreds of prophecies about the Messiah. It was clear that many of these were fulfilled in the New Testament. This process of discovery literally transformed my life.

Life Takes a New Direction

As the Scriptures took root in my life and I drew closer to God, my goal of becoming a millionaire by the time I turned thirty suddenly seemed insignificant. The treasures of this world became trivial as I understood the realities of His eternal plan and His call on my life. I knew God was calling me into full-time ministry, so after three years of pursuing my ambitions in business, I switched my major to the department of classics with a focus on religious studies and theology. After an additional three years of study, I was graduated with degrees in Jewish studies and early Christianity. Upon completion of my undergraduate studies, I started taking graduate courses and seeking the Lord about the next phase of my life.

Although God's calling on my life was certain, I still had no desire to go into full-time ministry. As a Jew, my only concept of "Christian" ministry was a Catholic priest, and to me this spelled commitment that included a vow of celibacy and perhaps even poverty. These were not options I could live with. But after much struggling—perhaps like Jacob's wrestling experience with God—and several more months of studying and prayer, I finally gave in to God's ultimate purpose for my life. I have walked with Yeshua ever since, and He has been beside me every step of the way.

Back in Rochester during a visit to my family in 1984, I attended a small Messianic fellowship of only five people. During the service, I had what can be described only as a vision where I saw the circular youth chapel of the church where our tiny group was meeting. It was packed with people worshiping in a Messianic service. When I went home that night, I could not sleep.

The stirring in my heart and mind was building to a conclusion, and by morning I knew that God was calling me to move back to Rochester and turn this little fellowship into a full-fledged Messianic Jewish congregation. I was to become a Messianic Jewish rabbi and reach out to my Jewish people with the message that Yeshua (Jesus) was our promised Messiah.

We called it Congregation Shema Yisrael. The Assembly of God graciously opened up its facility to us. What a great blessing to our small congregation! We remained there until 1988, when by the grace of God we were able to purchase our own building. The congregation grew into a healthy community of around two hundred Messianic believers and has continued to prosper to this day.

Distorted Teaching about the End Times

One Sunday during this time, the pastor invited a guest speaker to teach a seminar on the last days. The place was packed, which indicated to me there was great interest in this topic. I sat on the platform and listened as this teacher dressed in a fancy silk suit reported that the Third Temple had already been rebuilt in Jerusalem and that sacrifices would begin shortly.

Because I was already traveling to Israel regularly and had even lived there for a semester during my undergraduate studies to work on an archaeological excavation, I knew this was not true. I struggled to keep my composure as he continued to wow the audience with this fabricated and erroneous report. I watched the fervor of the audience build as they digested his false teaching.

As soon as the guest speaker finished, I spoke privately with the senior pastor. Together we confronted the man.

"The things you said today just aren't true," I said.

"Yes they are. I have pictures," he replied.

I asked him to show me the pictures, but he refused. When the senior pastor and I continued to press him, he relented, opened his briefcase and pulled out some photos that he said were of the rebuilt Temple. I recognized the photographs immediately. They were pictures of a conservative synagogue that had been constructed far away from the Temple Mount in the modern section of Jerusalem.

Since then I have listened and read many inaccurate and fabricated reports about a rebuilt or nearly rebuilt Temple. Most have been utter nonsense.

Why do I tell you this story? Because it is an example of distortions and misinformation that have been perpetrated upon God's people. Jesus told us to live in constant expectation of His return. This is a good thing. But He also said, "So if anyone tells you, 'There he is, out in the desert,' do not go out; or, 'Here he is, in the inner rooms,' do not believe it. For as lightning that comes from the east is visible even in the west, so will be the coming of the Son of Man" (Matthew 24:26–27).

Do Not Throw Out the Baby. . . .

For many years believers have viewed almost anything that happens on the international stage as a sure sign that the Second Coming is imminent. During the first Gulf War, some were declaring that Saddam Hussein fit the profile of the Antichrist. Prior to World War II, Adolf Hitler and Benito Mussolini were considered prime suspects. So was Josef Stalin. When Napoleon's armies swept through Europe, many were sure that he was the Antichrist.

Many men also have erroneously predicted the date of the world's end:

- In 960 Bernard of Thuringia, a German theologian, calculated that the end would come in 992.[1]

- Pope Innocent III (1161–1216), considered an intellectual and one of the greatest canon lawyers of his time, expected the Second Coming to take place in 1284, 666 years after the rise of Islam.[2]

- Augustinian monk and mathematician Michael Stifel (1486–1567), who discovered logarithms, calculated that the Day of Judgment would begin at 8:00 a.m. on October 19, 1533.[3]

- John Napier (1550–1617), Scottish mathematician, physicist, astronomer and astrologer who made common the use of the decimal point in arithmetic and mathematics, predicted that the world would end in 1688 or 1700.[4]

- Harvard University graduate, prominent New England Puritan minister, prolific author and pamphleteer Cotton Mather (1663–1728) chose 1697 as the year of Jesus' Second Coming.[5]

- A Baptist preacher named William Miller found an audience of thousands for his prediction that Jesus would return on October 22, 1844. When it did not happen, that day became known as *The Great Disappointment*.[6]

- More recently, Edgar C. Whisenant, a former NASA engineer and Bible student, predicted the "Rapture" would occur sometime between September 11–13, 1988. He published two books, *88 Reasons Why the Rapture Will Be in 1988* and *On Borrowed Time*. *88 Reasons* was extremely popular, with 4.5 million copies sold. The author gave away 300,000 copies to ministers throughout America. Some in the evangelical Christian community took the books seriously. When the prediction failed to occur, however, Whisenant wrote more datebooks, forecasting the world's end would come in 1989, 1993 and 1994. The rapture of the saints still had not occurred when he died in 2001.[7]

- Harold Camping spent untold millions on billboards that declared "Judgment Day" was May 21, 2011. Well, May 21 came and went, and here we still are. . . .

There have been countless others, of course, no one has been right so far. Jesus was very clear when he told us, "No one knows about that day or hour, not even the angels in heaven, nor the Son, but only the Father" (Matthew 24:36). Still, that does not mean we stop looking and expecting. He also said, "Therefore keep watch, because you do not know on what day your Lord will come" (Matthew 24:42).

Erroneous predictions have caused many to become disillusioned and throw out the baby with the bathwater. In other words, they have stopped looking for any signs of the Messiah's return.

And yet, He is coming, and I believe it will be very soon. In the pages ahead, I will tell you how I know.

2

Why Satan Hates the Jews

The first reason we can know the last days are near:
Satan is increasing his attacks on the Jews.

Historians and scholars who write about anti-Semitism often state that anti-Semitism is an illogical hatred of the Jewish people. I completely disagree. I think anti-Semitism is totally logical, systematic, deliberate and calculated. When we understand that at the root of anti-Semitism is Satan himself, it all becomes clear.

A vicious, bloody war is raging throughout the world. Although we cannot see it with our physical eyes, Satan and his hordes of demonic forces are fighting to retain control of this world.

Satan knows the clock is ticking and that the end is near. He is backed into a corner and striking out in any and every way he can. Spiritual warfare rages all around us. Whether or not we like or admit it, we are caught up in the midst of the battle. Satan is doing everything he can to rule over the hearts and minds of the human race. I believe his strategy has always been and still remains the same: to divide and conquer, and to convince people that God's word is not true and Satan is not real. And a major part of Satan's strategy is to focus on the complete and total annihilation of the Jewish people. He tries to accomplish this through the spread of anti-Semitism, and sadly, it seeped into Christianity early in its history.

A History of Persecution

There has never been a time in history when the children of Abraham have not been victimized. Since the day God called Abram to leave his parents and go to the land He would show him, the enemy has been hard at work to wipe out his offspring. Sadly, the Church became one of the primary perpetrators of this evil plot as they turned against the very roots of their faith. Look with me at a brief overview of the systematic, calculated and deliberate attempts to wipe out the Jewish people over the last two millennia of Christianity:

- AD 70—As many as one million Jews died when the Roman army destroyed the Temple and burned the city of Jerusalem.
- 1096 to 1270—Thousands—possibly hundreds of thousands—of Jews were massacred during the Crusades, including the entire Jewish populations of Prague and Cologne.
- 1182—Jews were expelled from France and their property confiscated.
- 1289—The council of Vienna ordered Jews to wear a round patch on their clothing.
- 1290—Jews were expelled from England.
- 1294—Jews were expelled from Bern, Switzerland.

- 1347—Thousands of Jews were massacred after being charged that they started the Black Death by placing poison in wells.

- 1400s to 1800s—The Spanish Inquisition, in which many Jews were forced to convert to Christianity by the edge of the sword, deported, tortured or killed, spanned 350 years. In his book *Our Hands Are Stained with Blood*, my friend Dr. Michael L. Brown writes that during the Inquisition:

> There was a witch hunt against baptized Jews who maintained any vestige of Jewishness! These Catholic Jews (called "Marranos," "Conversos" or "New Christians"), violently forced to convert in the first place, were carefully watched to see if they were practicing 'heresy.' Heretical practices included failure to eat pork; failure to work on Saturday; failure to wear one's best clothes on Sunday; keeping the biblical feasts; observing Jewish customs of any kind; saying any Jewish prayers; preparing food according to Jewish law; associating with non-baptized Jews; and intermarriage of children of Marrano families with children of other Marrano families. . . . Violators, or frequently those merely accused of being violators, would have property confiscated. They would be subjected to harsh confinement and horrible torture, leading to mock trials, degradation and often death at the stake.[1]

According to Brown, an estimated thirty thousand Marranos were burned alive, and many more were strangled after confessing to "heretical" behavior. In addition to this, in 1492, all non-baptized Jews were expelled from Spain.

- 1494—All Jews in the city of Trent, in Northern Italy, were massacred after a rumor spread that they had murdered a Christian boy for religious purposes.

- 1497—Jews were expelled from Portugal.

- 1826—Pope Leo decreed that Jews were to be confined to ghettos and their property confiscated.

- 1881–1921—During the late nineteenth century in Russia, so-called Christians massacred thousands of Jewish people in *pogroms*. *Pogrom* is a Russian word designating an attack, accompanied by destruction, looting of property, murder and rape, that is perpetrated by one section of a population against another. The Jews of Russia were the victims of three large-scale waves of pogroms, each of which surpassed the preceding in scope and savagery.[2]

Christian peasants would put crosses on their doors so the murderers would know to leave them alone. The pograms were thought to have been instigated as a result of a publication called *The Protocols of the Learned Elders of Zion* in the Russian newspaper *Znamya* ("The Banner"). It was represented as a series of articles in 24 chapters (or protocols), of the minutes of secret, conspiratorial meetings between a group of powerful Jewish leaders (called The Learned Elders of Zion), documenting their plans to dominate the world economically, manipulate the media and create religious conflict toward their evil ends.

It achieved the desired results, adding fuel to the fire of an already dangerously anti-Semitic situation. The pogroms against the helpless Jews living in the small villages grew increasingly more violent, causing a huge wave of Jewish emigration fleeing from Russia to America in the early part of the twentieth century with little more than the clothes on their backs. In 1921, the *London Times* presented undeniable proof that the *Protocols* was nothing more than a "clumsy plagiarism" of other works not even associated with the Jews.

The list of what the Jewish people have suffered could go on for pages and fill entire bookshelves. But despite these horrible injustices, and even though the land of Israel disappeared from the world map for centuries, the Jewish people maintained their identity. They did so despite threats by despots such as Pharaoh, Herod and Adolf Hitler, who was possibly the worst of them all.

Hitler was not some ancient barbarian running around in a loincloth slaughtering people with his sword. He was a barbarian all right. But he was an educated, modern man, surrounded by other educated men. Together they carried out the worst mass murder in human history.

The infamous Adolf Eichmann (1906–1962), sometimes referred to as "the architect of the Holocaust"[3] and who was hanged for his crimes in 1962, once said, "Throughout history men have dreamed of destroying the children of Abraham." True, but the question remains: *Why?*

The Serpent Is Condemned to Death in the Garden

In order to understand why, we must go all the way back to the beginning of Genesis, to the story of the creation of man.

God created the heavens and the earth. Then He created mankind and gave man dominion over the earth. I call this the principle of creation and delegation. God created man and put him in the Garden. God gave man the responsibility to be fruitful and multiply, to subdue the earth and have control over it (see Genesis 1:28). In essence, God handed over the title deed of this earth to Adam and Eve. The Fall described in Genesis 3 represents a transfer of that authority.

When Adam and Eve disobeyed God and ate from the tree of the knowledge of good and evil, they handed over the title deed of this earth to the serpent. The significance of this earthshaking event cannot be understated. It was a radical transformation!

31

Until this moment in time, there was no sin. There was no evil. No disease had access to the earth, so there was no death. There was no need for clothing, because there was no sexual impurity of any kind. There was no need for covering because man was in perfect fellowship with God and without sin. There were no weeds. It was a state of perfection and absolute paradise.

Man's act of disobedience brought a complete reversal to earth's balance. It turned God's creation upside down. The fruit of man's disobedience brought sin, death, corruption, murder, perversion and destruction to all life on earth.

But then God provided a glimmer of hope when he promised that He would bring division—enmity—between mankind and the serpent because of their conspiracy: *"And I will put enmity between you and the woman, and between your offspring and hers; he will crush your head, and you will strike his heel"* (Genesis 3:15, emphasis added).

In this verse, we find the Bible's very first prophecy, or promise, of the Messiah's triumph over Satan. Biblical scholars call this the *Proto-Evangelion*, which means "First Gospel." In other words, thousands of years before Yeshua came to proclaim freedom to those held captive by sin, God told Satan, *The day will come when your head will be crushed, and it will be through the seed of the woman.* Ultimately, the time would come in history when the woman's seed would crush the serpent's (Satan's) head—dealing him his final deathblow.

Since the moment God pronounced the curse on him, Satan has known his days are numbered—that he lives under a sentence of eternal death declared by God Himself. Naturally he has continued to do everything within his power to keep that sentence from being carried out.

It is important to note that God's promise was through the seed of the woman—not the seed of the man. This is highly unusual, since "seed" is always tied to the male. It is the male that fertilizes the egg with his seed in sexual union. But in this unique prophecy of the promised Redeemer, it is the "seed of the woman," not the seed of the man, as would be expected. The only explanation is that this Redeemer would be born of a woman, a virgin. It is a prediction of the virgin birth of the Messiah.

For centuries Jewish theologians have argued that the Christian interpretation of the Hebrew word *almah* (עלמה) in Isaiah 7:14 is in error. They argue that the word *almah* does not, in fact, mean "virgin," but simply "a young maiden of marriageable age." The prophecy in Genesis 3:15, however, is much older, and in my view, much clearer that *the seed of the woman* would eventually bring about the serpent's destruction by crushing his head.

Clearly, this astounding prophecy is a prediction of the eventual coming of the Redeemer, Yeshua HaMashiach ("Jesus, the Messiah"), who was born of the *seed* of the woman—born of a virgin.

So what does all this have to do with the Jews and Satan's efforts to destroy them? The answer lies in what I call the Seed Promise.

The Continuation of the Seed

The history that follows the Fall of Man is a sad one. Almost immediately we see the severity of disobedience. Adam and Eve most likely understood this promise of Genesis 3:15—the promise of a Redeemer who would turn everything back to the way it was—to be fulfilled in their firstborn son, whom they named Cain. Imagine their disappointment, horror even, and the agony they must have endured when instead of being the promised Redeemer, Cain became a murderer of his own brother, Abel. How they must have grieved when they realized that their exile would continue for the remainder of their lives!

The entrance of murder into the world through Cain demonstrates the severe impact of their fall in the Garden. What followed was tragic. We are told of a society that grew increasingly evil until God actually regretted that He had made man and placed him on the earth.

> The LORD regretted that he had made human beings on the earth, and his heart was deeply troubled. So the LORD said, "I will wipe from the face of the earth the human race I have created—and with them the animals, the birds and the creatures that move along the ground—for I regret that I have made them."
>
> Genesis 6:6–7

There are no sadder verses of Scripture in the entire Bible than these. Man's unbridled depravity, coupled with his senseless inhumanity to his fellow man, grieved God to the extent that He destroyed the earth with a flood, preserving only Noah, a descendant of Adam and grandson of Methuselah, and his family. After the flood God blessed Noah and his sons, saying, "And I, behold, I establish my covenant with you, and with your seed after you" (Genesis 9:9). The seed continued, because God declared it would.

We do not hear about this Seed Promise again until six chapters later, where we are introduced to a man named Abram. We are not told why God chose Abram or how God revealed Himself to Abram, but He did. And He made a demand and a promise to him:

> The LORD had said to Abram, "Go from your country, your people and your father's household to the land I will show you. I will make you into a great nation, and I will bless you; I will make your name great, and you will be a blessing. I will bless those who bless you, and whoever curses you I will curse; and all peoples on earth will be blessed through you."
>
> Genesis 12:1–3

Imagine being asked by God to give up everything familiar to you—your home, your extended family, your friends—and go into a foreign land that God did not name. This was a remarkable requirement that emphasizes why Abram (later renamed Abraham) became the father of the Jewish people and why he is one of the great men of faith listed in Hebrews 11.

God promised to bless the world through Abram—to bless those who bless him, and to curse those who curse him. This is a biblical decree that is just as valid today as it was when the Creator of the universe declared it thousands of years ago. History shows that God has blessed those who have blessed the Jewish people, and He has cursed those who have cursed the Jewish people. But more importantly, it is God's promise of blessing to the world.

Fulfillment of this declaration can be seen both physically and spiritually. First, the Jewish people have been a blessing to the world throughout their history. Although they represent only one quarter of one percent of the world's population—a true minority—Jewish people have disproportionately contributed to the great advancements of the world in medicine, science, literature and culture. Even more significant, however, is the spiritual fulfillment that all the families of the earth would be blessed through Abram's seed or lineage. The ultimate fulfillment of this promise is the provision of the Messiah, the Savior for all mankind, Jesus of Nazareth.

Christians often forget that it was the Jewish people who *established all the foundations of our faith.* Paul clearly lists these in Romans 9:4, when he says, "Theirs [the people of Israel] is the adoption as sons; theirs the divine glory, the covenants, the receiving of the law, the Temple worship and the promises." God provided all this through Abram's seed.

The point I am trying to make is this: Satan understood that the Seed Promise of Genesis 3:15—that God decreed the seed of the woman would ultimately crush Satan's head and bring about his destruction—now rested upon Abraham. This Seed Promise would continue through Abraham's physical descendants—the Redeemer would eventually appear through his line and, if not stopped, bring about Satan's destruction. So it is only natural that the descendants of Abraham would become his primary target to eliminate!

Anti-Semitism and attempts to destroy the Jewish people throughout history have been nothing more than Satan's attempts at self-preservation. His thinking has been simply this: *If I can destroy the descendants—the seed—of Abraham, the father of the Jewish people and the one whose lineage would produce the Redeemer, then I can keep Genesis 3:15 and my own destruction from happening.* Satan is the great deceiver, and he has deceived himself into believing that he can keep Genesis 3:15 and the decree of his own destruction from being fulfilled. His number one priority, then, has been to destroy the people of the seed. This is, I believe, the basis and rationale of all anti-Semitism. It is a logical, systematic and calculated effort orchestrated by Satan himself to destroy the Seed Promise and preserve his life. Destroy the Jews, destroy the seed. Destroy the seed, destroy the Redeemer. Destroy the redeemer, keep Genesis 3:15 from ever being fulfilled.

Efforts to Destroy the Jews throughout Biblical History

We have briefly discussed examples of satanic efforts to destroy the Jewish people throughout the history of the Church. But let's look back even further.

One of the clearest early examples is found in the second book of the Bible, Exodus. Some 430 years after Joseph's brothers sold him into slavery in Egypt, the Lord was about to raise up a deliverer to bring his descendants back to their Promised Land.

The hero, of course, is Moses, who represents a type of the Messiah. Throughout the Old Testament, there are types and shadows of the redeeming work that the Messiah would ultimately fulfill. Moses is an example of this typology. He was raised up by God to redeem the Hebrew nation.

Throughout biblical history, we see that as God prepared to redeem Israel, demonic opposition spiked, and dramatic efforts to destroy the Jewish people accelerated. During the time the Hebrews were in Egypt, Satan was determined to keep them in slavery, and ultimately to bring about their destruction. Pharaoh was his man—a type of antichrist. Satan implanted in him a hatred of the Hebrews, and upon hearing that a deliverer would be raised up from among them, Pharaoh ordered the systematic deaths of all male children. "Then Pharaoh gave this order to all his people: Every Hebrew boy that is born you must throw into the Nile, but let every girl live'" (Exodus 1:22). The enemy was in tune with God's timing. He knew of the prophetic or redemptive act with Egypt and raised up Pharaoh as his minion. Exodus 7:13 is the first of more than a dozen times where the Bible says "Pharaoh's heart became hard" or "was hardened" toward the Israelites.

You know the rest of the story. Moses was put in a basket and floated out on the Nile River. Pharaoh's daughter found him and raised him in Pharaoh's own palace. Indeed, the very person who sought Moses' destruction became his protector. Moses ultimately survived and led the children of Israel out of Egypt. Pharaoh, then, represents a spike, one of Satan's concerted historical efforts to keep the seed, Israel, from surviving. Every time God was about to perform another prophetic act, a *spike* in Satanic activity can be easily identified.

All Part of the Redemption Plan

Yet God's chosen people survived at terrible odds. Why? How? It is all part of God's plan of redemption.

Moses' floating in a basket down the waters of the Nile and being rescued by Pharaoh's daughter was a form of *redemption* for Israel. The exodus out of Egypt was *redemption* for the nation of Israel. Israel then survived repeated attempts at total annihilation as they attempted to reoccupy the Promised Land. Then Assyria attempted to destroy the Northern Kingdom of Israel in the eighth century BC, followed by the Babylonian captivity in 586. Each of these were systematic efforts to displace and destroy the children of Israel. God's *redemptive* promise, however, brought back a remnant from the Babylonian captivity that rebuilt the Temple and resettled in the Promised Land of Israel.

Then we have Haman's plot to murder all the Jews in the book of Esther (Hadassah in Hebrew). Risking her own life, Esther appealed to the king and rescued the Jews. This exciting *redemption* and victory over attempted annihilation became an annual celebration for Israel that is known as the Feast of Purim.

Israel continued to cry out for their promised Redeemer. As they later suffered under Roman tyranny, Messianic expectation permeated the air. Of course, Satan knew that a *redemptive* act of God was about to take place, so he used another antichrist figure, King Herod. Hearing about a long-awaited king, Herod summoned the wise men of Israel to learn where this predicted Jewish Redeemer would be born. The wise ones revealed an ancient prophecy of Micah: "But you, Bethlehem Ephrathah, though you are small among the clans of Judah, out of you will come for me one who will be ruler over Israel, whose origins are from of old, from ancient times" (Micah 5:2).

Herod responded by sending his army to destroy all male children under the age of two years. Although the gospels do not tell us how many innocent babies were murdered, how many mothers' hearts were shattered by this unspeakable cruelty, we do know that Yeshua was not among them. Matthew 2:13–14 records that an angel warned Joseph in a dream, and by the time Herod's troops reached the small and seemingly insignificant village of Bethlehem, Jesus, Mary and Joseph were well on their way to Egypt.

This slaughter of Israel's male children was another spike in demonic fervor to wipe out the Seed Promise of Genesis 3:15. Yet the Messiah and his parents fled to Egypt just in the nick of time and were thus spared from Herod's (Satan's) destructive plan. Again God *redeemed* the chosen seed of Israel.

Failing to kill the Messiah as an infant and not realizing that God had planned all along to offer Him as a sacrifice for our sins, Satan then convinced the Jewish and Roman leaders to condemn Yeshua to death. Can't you just picture the devil laughing as he watched our Messiah dying on that tree? What evil delight he must have felt, even as Yeshua quoted Scripture from Psalm 22:1: "My God, my God, why have you forsaken me? Why are you so far from saving me, so far from the words of my groaning?" Jesus was quoting Scripture, and once again, Satan's attempt to defeat God's purposes actually resulted in carrying them forward.

With the atonement and resurrection of the Messiah at Calvary, the Bible is clear that Yeshua defeated Satan and brought captivity captive, making an open show of this victory:

> Having canceled the charge of our legal indebtedness, which stood against us and condemned us; he has taken it away, nailing it to the cross. And having disarmed the powers and authorities, he made a public spectacle of them, triumphing over them by the cross.

> Colossians 2:14–15

After living a completely sinless life while battling this intense spiritual warfare that none of us can ever comprehend, Yeshua went in obedience to die on the cross, ultimately fulfilling His purpose to die for our sins. Although the physical agony of the crucifixion cannot be underestimated, it was the spiritual torment as God laid upon Him the sins of the world that must have been the most unbearable. The death of Yeshua rockets our minds beyond the realm of finite thinking.

It was the ultimate act of *redemption*.

Genesis 3:15—A Two-Part Fulfillment

I really do not think Satan understood or fully understands still how God's plan is going to work out. Otherwise, he would have focused all his efforts on stopping the crucifixion. He could not have comprehended what the death of Jesus would mean for him.

Yeshua's atoning death act at Calvary and resurrection three days later secured a definitive defeat over Satan. Yeshua has defeated him openly and now is above every principality and power. Every knee must bow and tongue confess that He is Lord. Spiritually, for those who put their trust in Him, all things are under His feet and therefore ours.

If Jesus succeeded in fulfilling Genesis 3:15 fully at Calvary, however, why does the history of intense anti-Semitism continue? If Jesus' death and resurrection at Calvary destroyed the serpent and crushed his head, then why do we continue to experience death and destruction? Why does evil continue to have such a hold on our world? Why do we have a two-thousand-year legacy of atrocities committed against the Jewish people, almost entirely at the hands of those who call themselves Christians? Just look around: It is evident that Satan is still alive and well and operating in the world today.

I have to conclude that the answer is that Genesis 3:15 has not yet been fulfilled. It is only the first installment. It has not yet been completed. Yes, Calvary was the down payment, but the Bible is clear that the enemy of death has not yet been con-clusively defeated. The rule or domain of Satan has not yet been brought to completion.

While the work of redemption has certainly begun, Genesis 3:15 is yet to be fulfilled in its entirety because it requires a Second Coming. The first time, the Lamb of God came to take away the sins of the world, but when He returns, He will come as the Lion of the Tribe of Judah in victory, power and judgment to destroy the enemies of God.

The fulfillment of Genesis 3:15, therefore, has to be a two-part fulfillment. Otherwise, why has Satan worked so diligently to destroy the Jewish people in the last two thousand years since Jesus came? Just as the Jewish people played a fundamental, foundational role in the Redeemer's first coming, they also play an equally significant and fundamental role in His return. Satan, therefore, continues to try to destroy them at all costs.

Running Out of Time

Although the enemy has failed miserably to thwart God's plan to bring His Redeemer into the world through the Jews, Satan will not and cannot surrender. The battle between good and evil is a fight to the finish . . . of the earth. Fully aware that his time is running out, Satan continuously steps up his efforts to escape the death sentence pronounced over him in the Garden. *I cannot reiterate enough that anti-Semitism is nothing more or less than Satan's attempt at self-preservation.*

It is not possible, therefore, to understand the last days with-out understanding Israel's role in all this. Israel is central to the return of the Messiah, through both their promised return to their land and their recognition of Him as their promised Mes-siah. Yeshua will not return until His Jewish brethren cry out, "Blessed is he who comes in the name of the Lord" (Matthew

41

23:39). Satan is doing everything possible to keep this from happening in order to keep the Messiah from returning.

I am convinced that the persecution of the Jewish people begins with Satan himself and always goes back to Genesis 3, the Fall of Man and God's curse on the serpent. The death sentence that God pronounced over Satan (the crushing of his head) sent him into action and brought about the logical, systematic, calculated plan to destroy the Seed Promise wherever and whenever it can be found.

If the Jewish people were not completely God's idea, they never would have survived the numerous attempts—by the Amalekites, Jebusites, Canaanites, Pharaoh, Haman, Herod and all the others—to wipe them off the earth. All these sought to destroy the Jewish people; they were all clearly vehicles of Satan. His motivation? It has to be the death decree described in Genesis 3:15. Satan has carried a death sentence from the Garden of Eden—he has always known he has an expiration date!

The Deception of Satan

The fact that Christians themselves have persecuted the Jewish people for so long has naturally created an added barrier for Jewish people to respond to the redemptive plan God provided through the atoning death and resurrection of Yeshua, who Himself said that He was sent to the Jews first (see Matthew 10:5–6, Matthew 15:24, Romans 11:11–15). The Church, over history, has adopted views such as Replacement Theology (the belief that the Jews rejected Yeshua, and therefore, Christians have replaced them as God's chosen people) and the concept of deicide (the idea that the Jews were responsible for killing Jesus and bear a curse for that act). Both of these will be discussed further in chapter 5. Make no mistake: This persecution by the Church is a calculated plan of Satan to misuse the very people who were commissioned to bring God's message of redemption to the Jewish people. Christians, therefore, have come to be viewed by many Jews as the greatest persecutors and haters.

Some people look at the unreasoning hatred directed at the Jews and say, "It makes no sense." But it makes absolute sense to me. Satan's tragic yet brilliant strategy is to use the very people who were to provoke the Jews to jealousy (Romans 11:11). He has used those who identify themselves as Christians to destroy the Jewish people in the name of Christ and Christianity.

The very dilemma we face today in sharing the Gospel with Jewish people is the result of this misconception. Have the Jews rejected the Gospel? No, they have heard a distorted message that they cannot possibly embrace: a "gospel" that Christians hate Jews and blame them for killing Jesus. In order for Jews to see the biblical truth that followers of Jesus do not hate Jews but have a biblical mandate to love them and to share their faith with them, we must overcome this misconception.

Do you see, as I do, that Satan's strategies have been successful in keeping Jews from embracing their Messiah? Do you see how the curse in Genesis 3:15 is at the very root of anti-Semitism? It all traces back to the Seed Promise and Satan's efforts to preserve his very life. It all comes back to Israel and their restoration. It is no accident that Israel's capital city, Jerusalem, is back in the hands of the Jewish people, where Jesus said He would come when the Jewish people, at last, will cry out to Him, "Blessed is he who comes in the name of the Lord" (Matthew 23:39; Luke 13:35).

The blindness, we are told, must come off of their eyes. Then ultimately all Israel will be saved.

> For I do not desire, brethren, that you should be ignorant of this mystery, lest you should be wise in your own opinion, that blindness in part has happened to Israel until the fullness of the Gentiles has come in. And so all Israel will be saved, as it

is written: "The Deliverer will come out of Zion, and He will turn away ungodliness from Jacob; for this is My covenant with them, when I take away their sins."

Romans 11:25–27, NKJV

In this passage Paul was referring to Isaiah 59:20–21 and 27:9, and Jeremiah 31:33–34. The Redeemer will come forth out of Zion and turn godlessness away from Jacob. The last days, therefore, cannot be divorced from the salvation of the Jewish people.

Satan failed miserably the first time Jesus came. Jesus' crucifixion was a setback for him, yet he remains on the loose and active, bringing deception, murder and violence to prevent Jesus from returning. In effect, Jesus remains in the heavens until the restoration of all things.

> Repent, then, and turn to God, so that your sins may be wiped out, that times of refreshing may come from the Lord, and that he may send the Christ, who has been appointed for you—even Jesus. He must remain in heaven until the time comes for God to restore everything, as he promised long ago through his holy prophets.

Acts 3:19–21

If you have eyes to see, you will understand that the backbone of the whole end-time scenario—the spinal cord, if you will—is the Jewish people. To Satan, they are the jugular, and Satan believes that cutting off the jugular leads to the death of God's redemptive plan. Israel's demise is the last piece of the puzzle. It serves as a gulf in Satan's mind that cannot be bridged. From the first century to now, Satan's primary target has been Israel and the Jewish people. He knows that when the Redeemer returns for His own, He will fulfill God's covenant promises to Abraham, and Satan will be destroyed.

If you understand this, you know what to look for in the last days. When you understand what Satan is trying to do and why—with Genesis 3:15 as the key—then you can fast-forward to the book of Revelation, identify Satan's targets and understand how he thinks. He is in the final battle to preserve his life. He is compelled to keep the Messiah from coming back and keep Genesis 3:15 from happening.

Yet all Satan's efforts to destroy the Jewish people—through Cain, the Canaanites, Pharaoh, Haman, Herod, the Romans, the Crusaders, the Spanish Inquisition, Hitler and even now Iran's Ahmadinejad—have failed and will continue to fail. For God's laws are higher and greater than all others. His Word will always prevail. His promise to preserve Israel continues to triumph to this day.

Israel, the land and the people, remain!

3

Aliyah: The Return of the Jews

*The second reason we can know
the last days are near:
Scattered Jews are returning to Israel
from the four corners of the earth.*

The first few books of the Old Testament are dominated by accounts of Israel's ancient enemies—the Amalekites, Hittites, Jebusites, Canaanites and so on. But when was the last time you saw anything about the Amalekites on the evening news? Those nations have vanished. Many people have never even heard of them. Yet the Israelites remain.

By man's logic, Israel should not exist. The often-scattered nation should have disappeared hundreds or even thousands of years ago. Yet despite being continually overrun by foreign oppressors and scattered throughout the world, they have survived.

Even before Israel was reestablished as a country in 1948, the dispersed children of Israel retained their heritage and cultural identity. The fact that they were not absorbed completely into the cultures of the nations that overtook them at various points throughout history is one of the great evidences of God's faithfulness. No other nation in history has ever survived without a country to call their own for so long. But God remained faithful to preserve them as a nation and declared that one day He would bring them back to their land:

> And it shall come to pass in that day, that the Lord shall set His hand again the second time to recover the remnant of His people, which shall be left, from Assyria, and from Egypt, and from Pathros, and from Cush, and from Elam, and from Shinar, and from Hamath, and from the islands of the sea.
>
> Isaiah 11:11, KJV

This amazing promise of returning the children of Israel, who have been scattered to the most remote corners of the earth, to their homeland is being fulfilled today. And this *aliyah*, or return of Jews to their biblical homeland, is yet another important sign that the Messiah's coming is approaching.

God Knows His People

In nearly every country of the world Jews can be found. We are a migrant people who have been scattered throughout the world.

When we think of the scattered tribes of Israel, most of us think of "The Ten Lost Tribes of Israel." These are the ten northern tribes described in the Old Testament—Reuben, Simeon, Dan, Naphtali, Gad, Asher, Issachar, Zebulun, Ephraim and Manasseh—that disappeared from the texts of the Hebrew Scriptures following the repeated invasions, victories, enslavements and deportations by the Neo-Assyrian Empire between

740 and 722 BC. The Southern Kingdom tribes of Judah, Levi and Benjamin are not included in this people group.

The Bible never tells us what happened to these people. They simply vanished or assimilated into the culture of their captors. Many of these groups, however, are now appearing in various parts of the world, claiming to be descendants of these ten lost tribes.

Then there was the Babylonian captivity. In 586 BC, the two remaining tribes of the Southern Kingdom, Benjamin and Judah (with many Levites mixed in), were taken captive by the Babylonians. Seventy years later a remnant of them returned to Jerusalem and rebuilt the Temple. Most Jews today trace their lineage back to the Southern Kingdom, since the word *Jew* comes from the inhabitants of Judea, which is the area surrounding Jerusalem.

The Bible is clear, however, that only a remnant returned. What happened to the rest? Along with the tribes of the Northern Kingdom, they were dispersed.

We also know about the dispersion of the Jewish people following the destruction of the Temple in Jerusalem in AD 70. The survivors of this Roman siege were scattered among the nations of the world. We refer to this today as the Diaspora, the scattering of the Jewish people throughout the nations of the world. And the dispersion did not end there.

Throughout the centuries, the Jewish people wandered from nation to nation as they were persecuted by their hosts. During the Middle Ages, Jews were forced out of England, Italy and France. They were expelled from Spain and Portugal at the end of the fifteenth century during what became known as the Spanish Inquisition. In later generations, they ran from the pogroms of Eastern Europe and the Nazis.

Where are all these Jews? First of all, they are not really lost.

Although many did assimilate into various cultures, not all did. Some preserved their identity in isolated communities.

I have traveled to more than fifty nations now, and in every nation I have visited, I have found Jewish communities in places such as Ethiopia, Zimbabwe, India, China and Siberia. In Ethiopia and Zimbabwe, for example, ancient Jewish communities have been found that practice a form of Judaism that predates Rabbinic (Talmudic) Judaism. Without understanding what they were doing, they have daily participated in Jewish practices and traditions about which they knew little or nothing. In truly the uttermost parts of the earth, thriving Jewish communities have retained their identities through the centuries.

These people are not lost. God knows where every last one of them is, and He is going to restore them. All these people are displaced—dwelling outside of their Promised Land. And God is committed to bringing them home to Israel.

Dreams and Visions in India

Recently, in the isolated states of Mizoram and Manipur, in northeastern India, I met with Jews who claim to be descendants of the tribe of Manasseh. They have been cut off from the rest of the world for hundreds of years. Their existence was not even discovered until the middle of the nineteenth century. There they were, hidden away, hundreds of miles from any outside influence. They are scattered throughout northeastern India, Burma (now Myanmar) and Bangladesh's Chittagong District. Until the last generation, they were animists. In other words, they worshiped the spirits of birds, tigers, trees, waterfalls and other aspects of God's creation.

These tribalists say that they had completely lost touch with their Jewish roots during centuries of exile in Asia. Yet they continued in certain traditions that traced back to their Jewish heritage without understanding the connection.

Then about 20 or 25 years ago some of their leaders began having dreams and revelations regarding who they were as a people. Initially they returned to the worship of one God, although they had no copies of the Bible. Many members of this tribe, particularly those living in the state of Mizoram, became Christians as the result of missionary efforts of the Presbyterian Church during the nineteenth century. Until about thirty years ago, they lived as Christians until their dreams revealed that they were, in fact, Jews. They reached out to members of the traditional Jewish community, and through this educational process many synagogues began to sprout up in both Mizoram and Manipur.

In an article written for the Jerusalem Center for Public Affairs, Nathan Katz and Ellen S. Goldberg wrote,

> No one knows quite what to make of these tribals . . . nor what to do about their claims to Jewish identity and their aspirations to immigrate to Israel. Several groups, especially Jerusalem-based Amishav, have made efforts to reintroduce them to Jewish observance, and some have undergone Orthodox conversion. The Israeli ambassador to Burma, Itiel Pann, is sympathetic to their cause, but the Israeli government recently denied visitor visas to a delegation of Indian tribals.[1]

The Israeli government may not know what to make of these people, but I do. As of this writing, nearly 14,000 of these Bnei Menashe have actually been allowed to immigrate to Israel, undergoing a simple ceremonial conversion process under the direction of the rabbinic community. Yes, God is calling His people home to Israel, even those who at one time did not even realize who they were!

Ancient Prophecies Are Being Fulfilled

Clearly, Isaiah, Jeremiah and other Old Testament prophets foresaw a time when the Jewish people would be gathered from the nations where they had been scattered and would return to the land promised to Abraham, Isaac, Jacob and their descendants. Today, this prophecy is being fulfilled at an extraordinary rate.

I led my first tour of Israel in January 1984. Our group of eighteen traveled the land on a minibus. We were in the Golan Heights when a woman asked our tour guide, "Why do you call this the *State* of Israel and not the *Nation* of Israel?"

Without even pausing to think about her question, our guide answered, "Because the *nation* of Israel is scattered throughout the world. And only when the people of Israel return in their entirety to the land of Israel will we call the *State* of Israel the *Nation* of Israel." In other words, the nation of Israel *is* the people of Israel, which includes those who are still scattered throughout the world. In fact, more Jews live in the United States than currently live in Israel.

An important distinction can be made between the geographical landmass that bears the name Israel and the people scattered throughout the world who make up the nation of Israel. The point could be made that Israel is the only nation of this sort in history. In fact, the only reason that this little sliver of land no bigger than the size of New Jersey is called Israel is because it was the land promised to the people of Israel. Without the people of Israel, the land is meaningless. The land and the people are forever bound together.

One of the great promises of the last days preceding the return of Jesus to this earth is the regathering of these scattered Jewish people (including those who live in the United States) who will one day be drawn back to their homeland. Am I saying that all Jews will return to the land of Israel before Jesus returns? No, but certainly a significant number will. This is a clear sign of the last days, and it is happening today before our very eyes.

God Always Keeps His Promises

"God is not a man, that he should lie, nor a son of man, that he should change his mind" (Numbers 23:19). One of the great attributes of God is that He always keeps His promises. He is steadfast—the same yesterday, today and forever. He does not change. He is faithful. Many passages of Scripture declare God's faithfulness, particularly in relationship to Israel.

> The LORD did not set his affection on you and choose you because you were more numerous than other peoples, for you were the fewest of all peoples. But it was because the LORD loved you and kept the oath he swore to your forefathers that he brought you out with a mighty hand and redeemed you from the land of slavery, from the power of Pharaoh king of Egypt. Know therefore that the LORD your God is God; he is the faithful God, keeping his covenant of love to a thousand generations of those who love him and keep his commands.
>
> Deuteronomy 7:7–9

> I brought you up out of Egypt and led you into the land that I swore to give to your forefathers. I said, I will never break my covenant with you.
>
> Judges 2:1

> Praise be to the LORD, who has given rest to his people Israel just as he promised. Not one word has failed of all the good promises he gave through his servant Moses.
>
> 1 Kings 8:56

I will sing of the LORD's great love forever; with my mouth I will make your faithfulness known through all generations. I will declare that your love stands firm forever, that you established your faithfulness in heaven itself. You said, "I have made a covenant with my chosen one, I have sworn to David my servant, 'I will establish your line forever and make your throne firm through all generations.'"

Psalm 89:1–4

For great is his love toward us, and the faithfulness of the LORD endures forever.

Psalm 117:2

God has declared with absolute clarity that Israel will continue as a nation and He will remain faithful to the Jewish people:

This is what the LORD says, he who appoints the sun to shine by day, who decrees the moon and stars to shine by night, who stirs up the sea so that its waves roar—the LORD Almighty is his name: "Only if these decrees vanish from my sight," declares the LORD, "will the descendants of Israel ever cease to be a nation before me." This is what the Lord says: "Only if the heavens above can be measured and the foundations of the earth below be searched out will I reject all the descendants of Israel because of all they have done," declares the LORD.

Jeremiah 31:35–37

The last time I looked, the sun was shining by day and the moon by night. Through these passages and many others God affirms His faithfulness to Israel. It is His proven faithfulness to Israel over the millennia that provides us with absolute confidence that He is and will remain faithful to us. He cannot turn His back on His covenant, because He would then be a liar and a promise-breaker in complete contradiction of everything we know about Him.

I remember a bumper sticker that read, "God said it, I believe it, and that settles it." This declaration speaks to what the Bible says about God's relationship with the children of Israel.

Is God Finished with the Jews?

If you grew up in a Christian home, you may have been taught that God finished with the Jewish people when they rejected Jesus as their Messiah. Nothing could be further from the truth! God has preserved the Jewish people not only because of His love for and faithfulness to Abraham, but also because Israel plays a vital role in His plan for world redemption. This includes both the First Coming and the return of His promised Redeemer, the Messiah.

Let us take a closer look at God's promises to the Jewish people:

> "The time is coming," declares the LORD, "when I will make a new covenant with the house of Israel and with the house of Judah. It will not be like the covenant I made with their forefathers when I took them by the hand to lead them out of Egypt, because they broke my covenant, though I was a husband to them," declares the LORD. "This is the covenant I will make with the house of Israel after that time," declares the LORD. "I will put my law in their minds and write it on their hearts. I will be their God, and they will be my people. . . . [They] will all know me, from the least of them to the greatest, declares the LORD. For I will forgive their wickedness and will remember their sins no more."
>
> Jeremiah 31:31–34

God acknowledges here that although the people of Israel have been rebellious and sinful, He will never reject them. In essence, He says, "I have the right to reject the Jewish people because of all they have done, but I will not. Period. Ever. Instead, I will give them a new and better covenant."

How can anyone read these passages with an open mind and believe that God has terminated His covenant with Israel? It simply is not possible.

Then in Romans 11:29, Paul reiterates God's promises to Israel from Jeremiah 31, pointing out that God's gifts and His call are irrevocable. Speaking of the Jewish people, he says:

> As far as the Gospel is concerned, they are enemies on your account; but as far as election is concerned, they are loved on account of the patriarchs, for God's gifts and his call are irrevocable. Just as you who were at one time disobedient to God have now received mercy as a result of their disobedience, so they too have now become disobedient in order that they too may now receive mercy as a result of God's mercy to you. For God has bound all men over to disobedience so that he may have mercy on them all.
>
> Romans 11:28–32

In context, Paul is teaching about God's faithfulness to the people of Israel. He declares three times in Romans 11 that God has not rejected them and never will. I have read this from every perspective, and there is simply no way to interpret this any other way than literally. Verse 28 says that they are enemies as far as their opposition to the gospel. This cannot be spiritualized. He is talking about the physical descendants of Abraham, Isaac and Jacob, the Jewish people!

Dozens of Bible passages clearly reveal the instrumental role of the Jewish people in the last days of the earth. Note the words of Yeshua Himself:

> O Jerusalem, Jerusalem, you who kill the prophets and stone those sent to you, how often I have longed to gather your children together, as a hen gathers her chicks under her wings, but you

were not willing. Look, your house is left to you desolate. For I
tell you, you will not see me again until you say, "Blessed is he
who comes in the name of the Lord."

Matthew 23:37–39

To whom is Jesus referring? He was clearly talking to the Jews
who lived in the city of Jerusalem at that time. Yes, many rejected
Him then, and many, out of blindness, continue to reject Him
to this day. But soon their blindness will be removed and they
will recognize Him as their Messiah. The prophet Zechariah
describes this in the most beautiful way:

And I will pour out on the house of David and the inhabitants
of Jerusalem a spirit of grace and supplication. They will look
on me, the one they have pierced, and they will mourn for him
as one mourns for an only child, and grieve bitterly for him as
one grieves for a firstborn son. On that day the weeping in Jerusalem will be great.

Zechariah 12:10–11

This prophecy cannot be fulfilled without a Jerusalem inhab-
ited by and under the control of the Jewish people. It would have
been impossible for this prophecy to see its fulfillment before
Israel was reestablished in 1948 and Jerusalem was recaptured
by Israeli forces during the Six-Day War in 1967. In Luke 21:24
Jesus declares, "They [Jerusalem] will fall by the sword and
will be taken as prisoners to all the nations. Jerusalem will be
trampled on by the Gentiles until the times of the Gentiles are
fulfilled." This is exactly what happened in 1967; after almost
two thousand years of Gentile occupation and control, the city
came back under Jewish rule. This was a direct fulfillment of
Bible prophecy and marked a transition point in biblical history.
It signaled the end of the time of the Gentiles and a return to
God's promised restoration of Israel.

4

Something Is Happening among the Jewish People

*The third reason we can know
the last days are near:
Many thousands of Jews are turning to Yeshua.*

The idea that the Jewish people all rejected Jesus as their Messiah is simply not true. The very disciples were Jews. It was Jewish believers who were responsible for taking the message of the Gospel to the nations of the world. The book of Hebrews was addressed to Jewish believers.

During the last two thousand years, there have always been Jewish believers. One of these, for example, Johann August Wilhelm Neander (1789–1850), son of a Jewish peddler, is considered among the Church's most revered historians. Baptized on February 25, 1806, Neander's divinity studies began at age seventeen. After being graduated from the university, he returned to Hamburg and became a Christian minister. Later called to serve the Church in Berlin, Neander was a prolific writer. The best known of his books, *General History of the Christian Religion and Church*, remains the greatest monument to his genius.[1]

Many Christians do not understand that it is often an extremely difficult decision for a Jewish person to accept Jesus as Messiah. It is not simply a matter of praying the sinner's prayer and then going on with one's life. It can mean that he or she is disowned by family and rejected by lifelong friends. They are labeled *meshumid*, traitors to their people and lost to Judaism.

And yet, despite the opposition they face, Jews are embracing Jesus as their Messiah in record numbers. This is perhaps the most noteworthy sign that we are in the last days.

Moscow 1994

I stood backstage in the middle of Olympic Stadium in Moscow in 1994, listening with my eyes closed as a chorus of voices lifted up songs of praise to God. I opened my eyes and gazed out at the near capacity crowd. The bleachers were filled with people. *The great majority were Jewish.* After I shared a brief Gospel message, I invited people to respond. When I looked out on the crowd, most of them were on their feet, signifying that they wanted to pray with me to accept Yeshua as their Jewish Messiah and Savior.

My mind raced back to the Bible's account of what happened on the Day of Shavuot (Pentecost), some two thousand years ago when the Holy Spirit was poured out in the Temple in Jerusalem. It was only fitting that this thrilling event in Moscow should be happening during this very feast. *Was this just a coincidence? Highly unlikely,* I thought.

Outside, Jewish *anti-missionaries*, many of whom had come all the way from the United States and Israel, were doing everything within their power to keep Jewish people from coming into the stadium. "Jesus is not for you!" they shouted at people making their way in. "These foreigners are apostates. They have ruined themselves with Christianity, and now they are trying to destroy you with it."

Their cries made little impact. Clearly Jews in the former Soviet Union were open to hearing what we came to share with them—that Yeshua could change their lives.

Spiritual Hunger in Russia

My call to Russia began while I was serving as a Messianic rabbi in Rochester, New York. After completing my college studies, the Lord had dramatically led me to my hometown of Rochester to begin a Messianic Jewish congregation. This was a bit of a challenge, because my unbelieving Jewish mother lived in Rochester, and she made it clear that this was the last place she wanted me to proselytize—as she put it—the Jewish community. It brings to mind Yeshua's words from Matthew 13:57: "Only in his hometown and in his own house is a prophet without honor." I experienced this firsthand.

In the early years of my ministry in Rochester, I invited a man named Jay Rawlings to speak to my small congregation. Jay was a freelance filmmaker who had produced a short film behind the Iron Curtain and managed to smuggle out the footage. The film was called *Gates of Brass* and recounted the plight of those who were known at the time as *refuseniks*.

Under Communist rule, Soviet Jews were not allowed to practice their faith. While many Russian Jews wanted to observe their Jewish identity and emigrate to Israel, the Communist authorities forbade them from doing so. Many had therefore lost their jobs or been kicked out of their homes. Some had even been put in *gulags* (prison camps) for trying to get their papers to go to Israel.

As I watched the film and learned about the plight of the refuseniks, I felt God's pain for these people. His heart was breaking for them, and He began to break mine.

God planted a seed in my heart, and from then on I had a growing desire to visit Russia and see what I could do to help. Finally this opportunity opened for me in 1990, when I was blessed to travel to Russia for the first time. As part of the Messianic Jewish Alliance of America (MJAA), I led a group of five other Messianic believers to distribute Messianic materials and gather information. We flew from Israel to Europe and then boarded the strangest plane I had ever seen, an old Russian Tupolev aircraft. We were scheduled to be there for only six days, had a list of five or six phone numbers but no official guide or contacts and basically had no idea what was going to happen when we got there.

We traveled lightly because we had to make room in our luggage for three hundred Bibles and three thousand pieces of literature about the Messiah. I remember asking one of our team members, "How in the world are we going to hand out three hundred Bibles in just six days?"

Yeshua had an answer to that. "Oh, ye of little faith" (Matthew 6:30, KJV).

And yet for the first couple of days after our arrival in Moscow, it seemed my lack of faith was justified. The phone numbers I dialed either were disconnected or no one answered. It was one dead end after another.

Then one of the members of our group had a revolutionary idea: "Let's pray." We all got down on our knees before God and poured out our hearts.

"Lord, we know You brought us here and that we are on a mission. Thank You for bringing us here to fulfill Your preordained plan. Lord, we need Your direction. Show us where to go. Open up doors for us to share our faith."

As we prayed, I felt optimism rising. God had brought us here to accomplish His purposes. All we had to do was trust Him. When we finished praying, I felt led to call one of the numbers I had tried several times before without getting an answer.

I slowly dialed the number. It rang once. Twice. Three times. I sighed and shook my head.

Suddenly I heard a *click*, and a man's voice came on the line. "*Slushayu vas*" (the Russian equivalent of "Hello").

I responded in English, explaining who I was and what I wanted.

"Yes, you have the right number," he responded in perfect English.

That person turned out to be our guide and translator for the rest of our time in Russia. Over the next few days I saw an openness to the Gospel the likes of which I had never seen in my ten years as a Jewish believer.

I remember walking into the street in a Jewish area with a bag full of Russian-language Bibles. We pulled out a few and offered them to those who passed by. You would have thought we were handing out hundred-dollar bills. Within two minutes we were surrounded by at least two hundred people, all clamoring for a Bible or a piece of literature. People were actually forcing others out of the way, fighting to get a copy of God's Word!

We let it be known that we were Jewish believers in Messiah, and word quickly spread. Over the next few days people actually took time off work and traveled two or three hours by train to get to our hotel so we could tell them about Messiah. It was awesome!

Those six days in Russia changed my life forever.

Within a month of returning to the United States, I received a call from the Messianic Jewish Alliance telling me it had received a phone call from a Jewish believer named Volodya. He lived in

Minsk, Belarus, some seven hundred miles from St. Petersburg. Somehow he had received one of the pieces of literature we had handed out and was calling the telephone number printed on the back.

He explained that he was a member of a group of about 75 Jewish believers, and they needed someone to come to Minsk and teach them more about Messiah and their newfound faith. He also told us that he needed training because he felt God calling him to reach out to his own people.

Over the next two years I made three trips to Minsk to work with this man and the other Jewish believers in his group. What a wonderful time we had together! We laughed. We sang. We held classes for the children and taught them the songs and dances of Israel. And we spent hours studying the Word of God, always coming back to biblical prophecies about the Messiah and God's plan for Israel. With excitement they would open their Bibles and show me where they had already underlined those passages. God had already spoken to them. I was just bringing confirmation. Clearly, this was a sovereign work of the Lord.

Volodya told me, "We saw from Romans 9, 10 and 11 that it is God's will for Jewish people to be saved, and this is possible only through Yeshua. Some people, Jews and non-Jews, think Jews can be saved another way, but this is not what the Bible says. There is only one way to God, and it is through His Son. This is the New Covenant in Jeremiah 31, is it not?"

He told me, "We want to worship God as Jews. In Romans 11, it says that 'all Israel will be saved.' It also says that Gentiles who are saved are grafted into Israel, so we are one in the Lord, even though we are different nationalities. Yet when the New Covenant came, the Jews stayed zealous for the law according to Acts 21:20."

The man's knowledge was amazing. No one had taught him this. Everything he knew came from his own reading of the Scriptures.

It was a glorious feeling to know that the Holy Spirit was moving sovereignly in the lives and hearts of Jewish people all over the former Soviet Union. And I was humbled when Volodya asked me, "Brother Jonathan, can you help us? How is it we should live as Jews who love Jesus?"

These were some of the greatest experiences in my life and ministry. It seemed that everywhere the Lord led me, I met Jewish people who were open to the Gospel. They asked me how they could know the Lord. It was a daily occurrence! Even the cab drivers. Nearly every time I boarded a taxi, the driver would be open to my sharing, and I would lead him to the Lord.

I could write volumes about the wonderful things I saw and experienced in the former Soviet Union over the next several years. It was a bit unnerving in that the conditions in which people lived were quite poor—far below what I was used to. Having no hot water for showers was common, as well as little or no heat during winter. We stood in long lines just to obtain one grocery item. Food was scarce, and I seldom had any idea what I was eating.

The constant surveillance by the KGB was unnerving at times. Beginning with our first visit to Moscow, it was apparent that we were being followed by various KGB operatives. On one occasion I saw them watching us from their car as we handed out Gospel literature. I walked up to their car and motioned for the driver to roll down his window. When he did, I handed him a couple of our flyers—one for him and one for his partner. He did not say anything, but he took them, and I trust that they bore fruit.

A New Calling

As I continued to travel back and forth, my burden for Russia grew. Up to this time, these trips had simply been a missions commitment. My primary responsibility was to Shema Yisrael, my own congregation in Rochester. As the burden grew stronger, however, I began to sense the Lord calling me to a greater commitment. I noticed that every time someone spoke about Russia or I heard the Russian language—even on television—I began to cry. I was becoming consumed with a desire to help these Russian-speaking people.

The fateful moment came while traveling on an airplane from Russia to a speaking engagement in Uppsala, Sweden, in 1992. I was passing the time reading the Bible and reflecting on all the wonderful things I had witnessed during my trip to Russia. I was reading Matthew 24, a chapter I had read many times.

In this passage Jesus answered two questions of His disciples. The first one involved time—when no stone will be left on another—which speaks of the destruction of the Temple and Jerusalem, a prophecy fulfilled in AD 70. The second question related to what signs would signal of the End of the Age. In other words, what were the signs of the last days?

I came to verse 14. Keep in mind, I am in Jewish ministry, and Matthew 24 relates directly to the prophetic destiny of Israel and the Jewish people. It was part of my text, if you will, for ministry. Although I had read this many times before, this time the verse literally jumped off the page at me: "And this Gospel of the Kingdom will be preached in the whole world as a testimony to all nations, and then the end will come."

It was a God moment!

As I sat on that plane, the Lord began to reveal things about this verse I had never seen. He drew my attention to the word *nation*. I knew from my studies that this word originated from the

Greek word *ethnos*, from which we derive the word *ethnic* and which literally translates to "ethnic group" or "people group." I saw this now in the light of Romans 1:16, that the Gospel is "to the Jew first, and also to the Greek." It suddenly became clear to me that the Gospel first had to go to every Jewish community in every nation where they have been scattered.

Although thousands of missionaries and evangelists had poured into the former Soviet Union by this time, little was being done to reach the huge Jewish community there. I heard the Lord clearly say to me, "Go back to Russia and reach My people." I knew immediately that this was not an invitation to continue the missions trips but to make a much more significant commitment to this land and these people.

Several months later, in obedience to what I heard the Lord say on that flight, I flew to St. Petersburg. I had no strategy, no real idea of what I was supposed to do other than what the Lord had spoken to me: "Reach My people."

I spent the following days meeting with spiritual leaders and looking at theaters and small halls to rent for some sort of outreach. A strategy began to form in my mind. My friend Alyosha Ryabinov and I traveled to Kiev together to meet his family and share with them. Alyosha had become an accomplished concert pianist, and while we were in Kiev he was invited to give a recital at his old music school. Around 150 people attended, including family, friends and members of the school.

Alyosha asked if I would mind sharing a little testimony when he finished the concert, and I agreed. I shared a little about myself and how I had come to know the Lord. I gave people an opportunity to respond, and to my surprise dozens actually responded to my message and prayed with me.

Afterward, one of Alyosha's cousins with a Ph.D. in physics began to argue with me. This brilliant woman in her midtwenties proceeded to present argument after argument as to why there cannot be a God. Finally I said, "I do not have an answer for all your questions, but I know that God loves you and wants to change your life." I watched in amazement as the Spirit of God came on her, and moments later I led her to the Lord. I may not be that smart, but it was obvious that God was up to something.

It was an amazing experience learning that salvation was not a formula of convincing proofs but was exactly as Paul said it was: "My message and my preaching were not with wise and persuasive words, but with a demonstration of the Spirit's power, so that your faith might not rest on men's wisdom, but on God's power" (1 Corinthians 2:4–5). I saw firsthand that God was moving in this dimension throughout the former Soviet Union. I knew that the Jewish people were hungry to identify with their Jewish heritage and connect with Israel.

Based on this understanding and past experience, I continued to look for halls to rent to host some sort of musical/cultural event in order to gain a platform for sharing the Gospel. But the more I looked the more frustrated I became. None of them seemed right.

Then, on the last scheduled day of my fact-finding mission to Russia, my taxi passed a magnificent white marble structure in the very center of the city. *Strange that I have never noticed this before,* I thought. I asked the driver what it was, and he said, "The Oktyabrsky Grand Concert Hall."

On impulse I asked him to turn around, and I got out of the car. Without invitation I knocked loudly on the back door. A secretary answered the door, and I asked if I could come in and look at the hall. She refused at first, saying it was an unusual request, but suddenly she changed her mind, saying, "Although this is highly unusual, come in."

I looked around and knew at once that it was the "Carnegie Hall" of St. Petersburg. Something leaped in my spirit. This was the place! I watched as God cut through the "red tape."

Within an hour I was meeting with the director of the hall, and by the time I left that afternoon I had secured the venue for three days in May with no deposit required. It all happened so fast! The reality that I had rented a four-thousand-seat auditorium did not hit me until months later. I had no money, no musicians and no experience whatsoever in event planning, but here I was.

People who know this story often comment, "What great faith you had!" Honestly, it did not feel like faith at all. It happened so quickly that I simply did not have time to realize what I had done until it was too late.

I took a sabbatical from my congregation in Rochester and moved into a dingy St. Petersburg hotel room near the concert hall to plan an event for which I had no previous experience. I spent the days—and then months—buying advertising, printing brochures and posters, renting hotel rooms—a myriad of details through which the Lord led me on a day-by-day basis.

Sometimes I felt like Abraham when God said, "Go to the land that I will show you" (future tense). This meant that Abraham must have awakened every day and asked the Lord, "Which way today?"

Messianic Festivals in Russia

When the doors opened on May 12, 1993, for our first International Festival of Jewish Music and Dance, nobody on my team—including me—had any idea what to expect. After all, Jewish people had been persecuted here for more than seventy years.

Many Jewish people had expressed fear about participating—or even being seen at such a visible event. Militant anti-Semites had always been a part of their lives in Russia, and they were afraid. To many Jews in Russia, Western Jews were unacceptable. And how would they respond to Jews who believed in Jesus? We had no idea.

To our surprise and delight, when the doors opened hundreds of people poured in, and literally within minutes the hall was filled to capacity. We were forced to shut the doors before the concert began and turn away hundreds of eager Jewish people who desperately wanted to get in. It was God's appointed time for the Jewish people in Russia—and it was unlike anything seen since that Shavuot almost two thousand years before.

The atmosphere that night was electrifying as Messianic singers and dancers ministered to the people. Then I shared a brief testimony of how Yeshua had transformed my life at age twenty and delivered me from drugs, the occult and other things in which college students like me were involved at that time. I explained to the predominantly Jewish audience that this was a Jewish message—that Jesus was not the God of Christianity, but was in fact the Messiah of Israel, promised by our own prophets. I told them of our separation from God, which is why Yeshua came to pay the price for our sins, and that His desire is to restore humankind to Himself. I challenged people to make a commitment by taking a step of faith—the same one I had taken years ago that transformed my life.

To our amazement, about 80 percent of the hall rose to their feet and began to pour down the aisles to the stage. I was overcome with emotion, and tears began to roll down my cheeks. I looked around and saw that many of our team members were sobbing as they watched something they had never imagined possible in our lifetime. Hundreds of Jewish people were responding to the Gospel at one time!

More than thirteen thousand people attended that first three-night festival, and more than 3,600 of those completed follow-up cards declaring that they had received Yeshua as Messiah. Of these, 2,350 were Jewish.

In the nights that followed we held follow-up meetings in another large hall. More than a thousand people came each night. We immersed several hundred of them in public baths in the days and months that followed.

Just a year later, we took a huge step of faith, and instead of renting a 3,800-seat hall, we rented Moscow's Olympic Stadium, which had a capacity of 17,500. Once again we experienced the same phenomenon, as not hundreds but thousands of Jewish people stood ready to pray with me and invite Yeshua into their lives!

Since 1993 our ministry has conducted these festivals in more than twenty cities throughout Russia, Ukraine, Belarus, Latvia, Moldova, Hungary and, in recent years, Argentina, Uruguay and Mexico. More than half a million people in all, including tens of thousands of Jewish people, have attended these festivals. Millions more have seen them on television. More than 250,000 have responded to altar calls to receive Jesus as their Messiah, and our conservative estimates confirm that more than 40 percent have been Jewish.

Look in the Mirror

During this time I traveled back and forth between the U.S. and Russia on a monthly basis. From the beginning it was clear that these hundreds of new believers would need to be discipled, and to do that effectively a Messianic Jewish congregation needed to be formed.

I prayed fervently for God to raise up a leader who would be willing to move to Russia. One day while I was shaving, I sensed the presence of the Holy Spirit speaking to me. He said, *There is no need to pray any more. I have found such a man.*

"Who?" I asked the Lord.

You are looking at him in the mirror, the Lord said.

I nicked my face with the razor in shock. It was me!

This was the moment of truth.

The ramifications of what God was saying to me at this moment were a bit terrifying. I knew the desire to go to Russia had come from God, because everything was going so well in my life and ministry at the time. I had every reason in the world to stay right where I was. Our congregation had grown from six founding members to more than 150 in just a few years. We had recently purchased our own building, and I had just bought a nice home. I was comfortable, well paid and surrounded by people I loved.

After several weeks of kicking and screaming, I finally decided to obey God. I met with the elders of Congregation Shema Yisrael and they affirmed the call. Thankfully we had an excellent assistant rabbi to lead the congregation. I gave notice to the congregation, put my house up for sale and began to give away many of my belongings.

In October 1993 I moved to St. Petersburg, Russia, and began to hold weekly meetings in what became the Messianic Jewish Center of St. Petersburg. A year later we began a full-time Messianic training center with more than 120 students, many of whom are currently in ministry. The congregation continues to this day, led by indigenous leadership. The Bible school and training center flourished and evolved into the Messianic Jewish Bible Institute (a combined effort of several Messianic Jewish ministries and churches) with schools all over the world, including Russia, Ukraine, Argentina, Brazil, Israel, Ethiopia, the United States and even Korea.

A Time of Miracles

I lived in St. Petersburg until 1997, and we continued to organize and conduct Messianic festivals throughout the former Soviet Union. God did so many amazing things during those glorious days. I could spend a lifetime filling books with my stories. Let me share just several with you briefly.

In 1994 we held a festival in Minsk, Belarus. Before the festival began, the authorities threatened to shut us down. There was no way I could obey their edict. That night such a huge crowd showed up that they could not all fit into the auditorium. They even had to shut down the metro stop near the hall because the crowds were so large. Our program went without a hitch, and hundreds prayed to receive Messiah. The following night the officials came sheepishly to us asking for tickets. We put them in the front rows, and one of the members of the religious committee actually accepted the Lord. As a result, our congregation in Minsk was allowed to operate, while others were forced to leave the country.

Everywhere we went in Russia, the Ukraine and other former Soviet republics, we saw an incredible openness to God. One day we stepped into a small Baptist church to speak with the pastor. While we were there a young man came in from the street to ask some questions about Christianity. It just so happened that he was Jewish, and we were able to share our faith in Yeshua. The pastor said to me, "He is not so unusual, brother. Jews in Russia also want to know the truth about God."

The miracle in the former Soviet Union was not that Jewish people were lining up to hear about Jesus. The miracle was that the bias among Jewish people in the United States did not exist there. Jewish people were willing to come to our events, knowing they would hear why we believed Jesus was the Jewish Messiah.

In each city of Eastern Europe where we brought the festivals, among the most moving experiences for me was the opportunity to minister to Holocaust survivors. With each festival, we organized a special reception for Holocaust survivors and then seated them in a special section. In the years between 1993 and 2000 when the festival ministry was at its height, we literally filled football stadiums. At each event, dozens of Holocaust survivors accepted the Lord.

The faces of these precious people who had suffered so much are permanently imprinted in my mind. I will never forget them and their tear-filled eyes as they stood to their feet to receive their Messiah. It is probably one of the most rewarding single experiences of these festival ministries.

We Encounter Anti-Semitism

The Moscow Festival in 1994 was so successful that we decided to return the following year. By 1995, however, things had begun to change: Moscow had become more Westernized and the city more violent. We had to hire private security on the streets because many anti-Semites were threatening us.

At one street performance in Moscow, passersby seemed genuinely interested in what we had to say until they discovered that we were Jewish. Then they turned on us.

"Jews, go home!" some shouted.

A stooped, gray-haired *babushka* ("grandmother") screamed, "I hate Jews! You should all burn in hell for what you have done!" She tore the invitation she had been given into little pieces, threw them on the sidewalk and then spit on them to show her disgust.

Another frail old woman yelled, "A festival for Jews? You Jews are pigs! You are devils!"

The unreasoning hate on their faces was a horrible thing to see. It was easy to imagine the wave of anti-Semitism that had swept Adolf Hitler into power nearly sixty years before.

One member of our group, a young Gentile woman from Maryland, was punched in the jaw, backed against a wall and spat on. Another woman tried to hand a man a tract, only to have him throw it on the ground and yell, "Heil Hitler!"

Her response was a firm, "God bless you."

The enemy was not amused that we had come into his territory to share the Gospel with the Jewish people. In fact, he was furious. But he could not stop us!

Jews Coming to Faith in Yeshua

All over the world Jewish people are coming to faith in Yeshua. Thousands are coming to the realization that choosing to follow Jesus does not mean they are converting to another religion and rejecting their Jewish heritage. They are realizing that it is possible to believe in Yeshua and remain a Jew. This is yet another sign that the last days are upon us.

Fifty years ago not a single Messianic Jewish congregation existed anywhere (there were only a handful of Hebrew Christian groups), and very few Jews professed faith in Yeshua—several thousand at best. By 2012, more than 500 Messianic Jewish congregations existed around the world, including at least fifty in Israel.

According to a nationwide survey, at least one million Jews in the United States have some sort of faith in Yeshua. This does not necessarily mean that they acknowledge Him as Lord and Savior. It does mean that at the very least they acknowledge Him as a divinely inspired teacher or prophet. Their eyes are being opened as Romans 11 foretold would happen.

Conservative estimates indicate that the number of Jews who believe in Yeshua, either in Messianic Jewish congregations or in believing churches, range somewhere between 50,000 and 100,000 in the United States and 250,000 to 500,000 worldwide. An estimated 20,000 Messianic Jews live in Israel today, and many of these were Jews from the former Soviet Union who now profess faith in Yeshua.

For the most part, the international media has ignored this phenomenon. This is understandable, but what is not is that many in the Church, including teachers, historians, evangelical and charismatic leaders, have ignored this as well. Yet it is one of the great miracles of our time and a clear sign of the last days.

The New Covenant

Let us look again at the promise of the New Covenant that God made to the Jewish people in Jeremiah 31:31–34.

> Behold, the days are coming, says the LORD, when I will make a new covenant with the house of Israel and with the house of Judah—not according to the covenant that I made with their fathers in the day that I took them by the hand to lead them out of the land of Egypt, My covenant which they broke, though I was a husband to them, says the LORD. But this is the covenant that I will make with the house of Israel after those days, says the LORD: I will put My law in their minds, and write it on their hearts; and I will be their God, and they shall be My people. No more shall every man teach his neighbor, and every man his brother, saying, "Know the Lord," for they all shall know Me, from the least of them to the greatest of them, says the LORD.

For I will forgive their iniquity, and their sin I will remember no more.

NKJV

Jeremiah was written at a time when the children of Abraham were divided into two groups: the ten kingdoms of the north and the two kingdoms of the south. Yet Jeremiah included all twelve tribes in the promise of this New Covenant. Paul tells us that the Gospel is to the Jew first (see Romans 1:16), and the reason for that can be traced back to this passage in Jeremiah 31.

So the promise of the New Covenant was made first with the Jewish people. We are then told it would be unlike the Mosaic Covenant, which they had repeatedly broken. God recognized their failure to keep the laws of Moses. Despite this, rather than reject them, which is what Replacement Theology teaches, He promised them a New Covenant that would give them something better. The text then lists four elements of this New Covenant that I want to enumerate:

First, we are told that in this New Covenant, *God would write His laws on our minds and hearts.* Whereas the covenant made with Moses was written on tablets of stone, this New Covenant would be internalized; it would be within.

I occasionally hear the accusation that Messianic Jews and Christians who want to observe their Jewish roots are putting themselves under the law by observing Shabbat and the feasts of the Lord such as Passover. "We are no longer under the Law," they argue. I agree, we are no longer under the Law. But what does this mean? Does it mean the Law has been eradicated? Has the Law been done away with, simply erased? Not at all. God has removed the Law from our shoulders, from the external, and placed it in our hearts. We now have the power to keep God's laws through the indwelling of His Holy Spirit.

Growing up in a Jewish family, I was taught the Ten Commandments at an early age. Yet only when I became a believer in Messiah at age twenty did the commands of God take root in my life. Why? Because the laws of God that were external to me before had now been written in my heart through the Holy Spirit. This is what happens to every true believer in Messiah. They have come into the glorious New Covenant and the external has become internal.

Second, the Mosaic covenant was about corporate relationship more than individual relationship. The Israelites saw God's might and power, but they did not have a personal relationship with Him in the sense the New Covenant offers. God was distant. He covered Mount Sinai, but the people could not touch the mountain or they would die. Their only access to Him was through Moses. Later, He dwelled in the Holy of Holies in the Tabernacle on the journey to the Promised Land, and later in the Temple at Jerusalem. But only the high priest—once a year on Yom Kippur, the Day of Atonement—could enter into this exclusive area.

By contrast, the New Covenant offers a living, breathing relationship with God. "I will be their God, and they will be my people" is a promise of adoption and inheritance. It speaks of an intimacy where He is no longer *Adonai* (literally "Sir" in Hebrew) or *HaShem* (literally "the Name") but is now *Abba*, "Daddy." It is about knowing Him personally, not just knowing about Him.

I am sure you have heard people say, "We are all God's children." In fact, that is biblically incorrect. This is made clear in John 1:12, where we are told that by receiving Him, He gave us the right to become children of God. This is an adoption that takes place through spiritual rebirth. This is the revelation that under the New Covenant, we are adopted. He becomes our God, and we become His children. We now can know Him personally.

I spent a lot of time learning *about* God when I was a child. I heard all the amazing stories about the miracles He had performed through the heroes of the Bible. I learned how He parted the Red Sea, gave the children of Israel manna in the wilderness, saved Daniel from the lions' den, etc. It was not much different from what I learned in school about George Washington and Abraham Lincoln. I knew George Washington was the first president of the United States and that he was often referred to as the "Father of Our Country." I knew Abraham Lincoln had freed the slaves, preserved the country during the Civil War and was assassinated by John Wilkes Booth. But I never felt that I *knew* Washington or Lincoln, and neither did I feel that I *knew* God.

But when I asked God to forgive me and invited Yeshua to come into my life, I discovered I could have an intimate friendship with the Creator of the universe. Now I do not just know *about* God. I know Him personally.

Third, we are told that a day is coming when "they will all know me, from the least of them to the greatest" (Hebrews 8:11). While the first two have already come to pass through the life, atoning death and resurrection of Yeshua, this third promise has yet to be fulfilled. It speaks of a time when all Israel—every man, woman and child—will know the Lord in this personal, intimate way. This is happening slowly as the blindness comes off the eyes of the Jewish people . . . and it must happen before Jesus can return. The apostle Paul, referring to the promise in Jeremiah 31, says it this way in Romans 11:26: "And so all Israel will be saved."

While thousands of Jewish people believe in Jesus today, it is still only a remnant. People often ask me if this verse means that every last Jewish person will be saved. To be honest, I do not know. But what I do know is that there is a set time in history when the vast majority of the physical descendants of

Israel who are living at that time will recognize Jesus as Yeshua, their Messiah. This is what I live for. My life's calling is to see the salvation of Israel, and I believe that day is coming soon.

The forgiveness of sin is the fourth element of the New Covenant: "For I will forgive their iniquity, and their sin I will remember no more." Under the Mosaic Law there was no real forgiveness of sin. Instead, yearly sacrifices were required in order to push the debt forward for another year. You might think of it as a balloon payment on a mortgage: You can delay payment for a while, even for many years, but sooner or later it comes due.

The sacrificial system covered sin in order to allow a holy God to dwell among His people. But the blood of Yeshua cancels sin forever. The slate is wiped clean. "If we confess our sins, he is faithful and just and will forgive us our sins and purify us from all unrighteousness" (1 John 1:9). This is the forgiveness provided for us through the atonement of Yeshua. As we are told in 2 Corinthians 5:21, "He made him who knew no sin to be sin for us, that we might become the righteousness of God in him." Through the Messiah, the Gentiles have now inherited this wonderful forgiveness of sin and the blessings of the New Covenant listed in Jeremiah. But the blessings were originally given to Israel, and one day the Jewish people as a nation will experience this forgiveness of sin once and for all. And this promise will be fulfilled in the days preceding the return of Jesus to the earth.

Grafted In

Again, the promise of the New Covenant was first given to the children of Israel. Gentiles who accept Jesus as Lord and Savior are "grafted in," and as grafted-in branches, they become partakers in all the blessings promised by God to the Jewish people.

"Some of the branches have been broken off, and you, though a wild olive shoot, have been grafted in among the others and now share in the nourishing sap from the olive root" (Romans 11:17). The olive tree refers to the covenantal people of God, the commonwealth of Israel. Now, through faith in Israel's Messiah Yeshua, Gentiles become spiritual sons and daughters of Abraham.

Jesus was born a Jew of Jewish parents in the Jewish homeland of Israel. Growing up, He lived as the Jewish people of His day lived, following the Jewish laws, rituals and customs of the Torah. He began His public ministry by proclaiming Himself to be the fulfillment of Isaiah 61, a prophecy heralding the Messiah who was to come. His disciples were all Jews, and His ministry on earth was devoted almost entirely to proclaiming the Good News to His own people. Jesus Himself said that He was sent only to the lost sheep of the house of Israel (see Matthew 15:24).

I don't want you to misunderstand what I am saying here. Yeshua came to die for all mankind. "For God so loved *the world* that He gave His only begotten Son, that *whoever* believes in Him should not perish but have everlasting life" (John 3:16, NKJV, emphasis added). "Whoever believes" is everyone, Jew and Gentile. But He came first for His own people, His own brethren, the people of Israel. And He was devoted to that task while on earth.

As a Jewish believer, I am saddened to meet Christians who could not care less about the Jewish roots of their faith or who see the Old Testament simply as a book of history with little or no relevance for them. Even worse, though, is when well-meaning Christians tell me, "Brother, you have become a Christian now—you are no longer a Jew." No, I am still a Jew. Like those first believers, I have found the One our prophets spoke of, and He is the Messiah of Israel. Jews do not have to leave their ethnic heritage when they accept Yeshua.

Reclaiming the Jewishness of Jesus

Another interesting development worth noting is that in recent years the Jewish community has reclaimed the Jewishness of Jesus. Although this is far from accepting Him as Messiah, Jewish leaders are recognizing that Jesus was a Jew and the importance of that fact.

Christian leaders, too, are recognizing that Jesus cannot be separated from His Jewish heritage. The March 18, 2008, issue of *Time* magazine featured an article entitled "Ten Ideas That are Changing the World." In it, writer David Van Biema introduced two American Protestant leaders—a Methodist New Testament scholar and a pastor of a megachurch—who regard sources like the Mishnah (a collection of early oral interpretations of the Scriptures compiled about AD 200 that make up the first section of the Talmud) and Rabbi Akiva (an authority on Jewish tradition who compiled much of the Mishnah and is considered one of the earliest founders of rabbinical Judaism) as vital to understanding history's best-known Jew: Jesus.

Van Biema called this dialogue "seismic." He said that some of today's Christian seminaries are actually teaching that one cannot understand Jesus outside of a Jewish context:

> The shift came in stages, first a brute acceptance that Jesus was born a Jew and did Jewish things; then admission that he and his interpreter Paul saw themselves as Jews even while founding what became another faith.
>
> Ideally, the reassessment should increase both Jewish-Christian amity and Gospel clarity, things that won't happen if regular Christians feel that in rediscovering Jesus the Jew, they have lost Christ. Yet [the pastor of the megachurch] finds this particular genie so logically powerful that he has no wish to rebottle it. Once in, he says, "You're in deep. You're hooked. 'Cause you can't ever read it the same way again."[2]

Romans 11:25–26 explains that Israel will experience a blindness until a set time in history when "the fullness of the Gentiles" comes in but reveals that following this, the day will come when "all Israel will be saved" (NKJV). Many Bible teachers mistakenly interpret *fullness* as "full number," as if some quota of Gentiles must first be saved, and then God will turn to the Jewish people when this number is finally reached. This is not my understanding.

The word *fullness* in the Greek is *pleroma*, and while this can refer to "full number," it is also defined as "fullness." I believe Romans 11:25–26 is saying that the Church must return to the fullness of its identity, including the variety of different restorations it has experienced and is currently experiencing. This includes a restoration of unity and the power of God. But one of the most important of these is a return to the Jewish roots of our faith.

I think the trend by both Christians and Jews toward reclaiming the Jewish identity of Jesus is noteworthy and plays a part in this pleroma, or fullness, that must be experienced before the blindness is completely removed. While this is still a long way from all Jews embracing Jesus as their Messiah, it is a start. In the words of songwriter Bob Dylan, "The times they are a-changin'."[3]

The Time to Favor Zion Has Come

One of the most important points I want to make in this book is this: *There is a direct connection between the salvation of Israel and the return of Jesus to this earth.* In fact, the turning of the Jewish people to Jesus and embracing Him as their Messiah and the fulfillment of God's promise that all Israel will "know me, from the least to the greatest" (Jeremiah 31:34) is probably the greatest single sign that we are truly in the last days and Jesus is soon to return. Many events and signs that are today connected with the last days are debatable, but this one is not. The Jewish people must recognize and embrace Yeshua.

"Fullness" in Romans 11:25 also refers to the fullness of time. Just as God had an appointed time to pour His Spirit on those gathered in the Temple almost two thousand years ago on Shavuot (Pentecost), He has a preordained, established time to fully restore Israel as a nation to Himself by removing their blindness. Yes, God has a set time to favor Zion. And I believe that time is upon us now. The blindness is coming off the eyes of the Jewish people. Since 1967, there are more Jews who believe in Jesus than at any time since the first century.

I sometimes hear excited Christians say that Jesus can come back at any time, at any moment. I am afraid this is not correct. Yes, He is coming soon. But He simply cannot come back until He is invited back by His Jewish brethren. There is only one Redeemer, and He shall come forth out of Zion. He is not returning to New York, Paris, London, Rome or any other great world capital. He is returning physically to Jerusalem! And that will only happen when Israel cries out to Him, "Blessed is he who comes in the name of the Lord" (Matthew 23:39).

I realize that you may be among those who believe that before God returns to the Jewish people in any great measure, the Church will be raptured and off the scene. I am not going to debate that topic because it is not the purpose of this book. I do want to point out again that regardless of your eschatology and where you place the Rapture, Jewish people are being saved today in greater numbers than at any time since the first century. The blindness *has already begun* to be removed from the eyes of Jewish people.

No one can be sure of the exact number of Jewish people who now believe in Yeshua, but I can tell you that in our ministry alone I have witnessed firsthand thousands of Jewish people responding to the Gospel over the last twenty years.

The time to favor Zion has come, and it is a clear sign, perhaps the clearest, that we are in the last days and that the coming of Jesus is drawing near.

5

The Gospel to the Nations

*The fourth reason we can know
the last days are near:
The Gospel is being preached to the nations.*

"And this Gospel of the Kingdom will be preached in the whole world as a testimony to all nations, and then the end will come."

Matthew 24:14

I consider the above statement, made by Jesus Himself, to be the clearest and most concise prophecy in the entire Bible concerning the last days. First, He directly mentions the end and connects it to the proclamation of the Gospel to the world. Put another way, He is saying that visible, worldwide evangelism will be the event or activity that will signal the last days are upon us. Second, He is laying out a chronology. The Gospel must first be preached throughout the world, and then, only after this happens, the end will come. I think it is fair to say that until this is fulfilled, the end cannot come, Jesus cannot return. So what does this mean? What is Jesus saying?

In the last chapter, I described the experience I had while flying from the former Soviet Union to a speaking engagement in Uppsala, Sweden. You will recall that as I was reading Matthew 24, which talks about the last days and Messiah's return, I had an encounter with the Holy Spirit. My attention became focused on a single verse, verse 14. I then was drawn to a single word—*nation.*

From earlier studies I knew both the Hebrew and Greek translations for this word. In Hebrew, *nations* is *goy* ("Gentiles"), and *goyim* is the Hebrew word for "people of the nations." The Greek word for nations is *ethnos*, from which we derive the word *ethnic.*

For most of us, the word *nations* brings to mind landmasses set apart by geopolitical boundaries established by man. Yet the word used in this passage of Scripture, *ethnos*, literally means "race, tribe," or as we more commonly say today, "people group" or "ethnic group."

In nearly every country of the world a wide variety of people groups can be found—including the Jews. As we discussed in chapter 3, we are a migrant people who have been scattered throughout the world. From the ten Lost Tribes taken captive during the Assyrian invasion of 722 BC to the Babylonian captivity in 586 BC, to the dispersion of Jews following the destruction of the Temple in AD 70, to the Jewish people at the end of the fifteenth century who were forced to scatter because of the Spanish Inquisition, to the pogroms of Eastern Europe and the Nazis in the last century, even to the persecution and subsequent dispersion brought about by some nations today, the Jews have had to make their homes in foreign lands throughout the world. The Greek word *ethnos* today, then, refers to the plethora of distinct people groups that dwell in every nation.

The United States alone is a melting pot for a myriad of nations (ethnic groups) that have settled here to find freedom. Italian and Greek communities thrive here, as well as Irish, Chinese, Puerto Rican, Indian, Persian, Arab, Cuban—the list goes on and on. Indeed, every people group under the sun is represented in the United States, and many of them have retained their distinctive characteristics—their houses of worship, languages, cultures, ethnic foods, etc. And one of these is the Jewish community. Although they have known great affluence here in the United States, the estimated six million American Jews still retain distinctive ethnic characteristics, including houses of worship and internal communication vehicles.

When Jesus said that the Gospel of the Kingdom must be preached to every ethnos, He was not saying that we had to reach only geopolitical countries, but that we had to reach the distinct ethnic groups that live within those countries. What a calling this is in the U.S. alone!

When you couple this with what Paul tells us in Romans 1:16, that the Gospel is "to the Jew first" and then to the nations (goyim or ethnos), we see the priority to take the Gospel to every Jewish community in every country where the Jewish people have been scattered.

I call this the missing link in missiology or world missions. Reaching the Jewish people is a key (if not *the* key) to reaching the nations. In Romans 11:11–15, we are told that Israel's rejection of Jesus as their Messiah has now caused the Gospel to go to the nations (ethnos):

Again I ask: Did they stumble so as to fall beyond recovery? Not at all! Rather, because of their transgression, salvation has come to the Gentiles to make Israel envious. . . . For if their rejection is the reconciliation of the world, what will their acceptance be but life from the dead?

What a blessing this is for those who were not born Jewish. But if that was a blessing, how much greater a blessing is in store when they (the Jews) come back. We are told it will bring *life from the dead*. This verse and others reveal that there is a linked destiny between Israel and the Church and between Israel and the nations. Just as Israel's rejection released the Gospel to spread throughout the world, so will their return release something in the heavenly realms that will have a profound effect on the remaining population of that nation. I do not understand how this works in the natural, but I am absolutely convinced that this is a spiritual reality.

This is happening now. Believers are reaching out to the nations, including the Jews, in countries around the world. Our ministry, Jewish Voice Ministries International, proclaims the Gospel to the Jew first, and also to the nations around the world. We've been holding huge events, such as medical clinics in impoverished nations and music and dance festivals in concert halls and stadiums in eastern Europe and Central and South America. Thousands of Jewish people are coming to faith. We are also equipping the Church to effectively share their faith with their Jewish friends. God has raised up other ministries similar to ours that are also reaching out to the Jewish people.

More Can Be Done!

Yet from my observation, the Jewish people scattered throughout the world (somewhere between 15 and 18 million) are being reached only by a small number of ministries whose message is focused toward them. This is of particular concern not only because the Jewish people need to hear the Good News (as do all people), but also because God has placed a top priority on reaching the Jewish people with the Gospel in these last days.

While it is true that technology is making it possible for the Gospel to be preached to people even in the remotest areas of the planet, which I see as part of the fulfillment of this verse, most Jewish people need specialized ministry in order to be effectively reached with the Gospel. A co-worker in Jewish ministry once put it this way: Just as a missionary has to travel overseas to reach people in other countries and then speak in their language so they can understand, we in Jewish ministry need to travel over a sea of misunderstanding in order to reach our people. And we then have to speak to them in their language so they understand. This is so true. We have to overcome a two-thousand-year legacy of hatred, persecution and misunderstanding to reach the Jewish people. And we need to speak in a language they can understand. When a Jew hears the name *Jesus*, they do not hear "Savior"; they hear "Christian God." When a Jew hears the word *convert*, they do not hear "repent and turn to God"; they hear "leave my Jewish heritage and accept another religion."

A Dual-Pronged Outreach in the First Century

Only after the Jewish communities of the world are reached with the Gospel will the Messiah be able to return. *"And this Gospel of the Kingdom will be preached in the whole world as a testimony to all nations, and then the end will come"* (Matthew 24:14). Here we have a black-and-white, crystal-clear statement from Jesus Himself that the Gospel must go to the ethnos of the world before He can return! This means to the Jew first!

In the first century, there was a dual-pronged ministry to proclaim the Gospel to both the Jews and the Gentiles. Paul tells us:

> On the contrary, they saw that I had been entrusted with the task of preaching the gospel to the Gentiles, just as Peter had been to the Jews. For God, who was at work in the ministry of Peter as an apostle to the Jews, was also at work in my ministry as an apostle to the Gentiles.
>
> Galatians 2:7–8

We can see from these verses that the Lord had called anointed leaders like Peter (James, John and most of the other apostles) to focus their outreach efforts on their Jewish brethren while Paul, Barnabas, Timothy and others were called simultaneously to go to the Gentiles. I believe God is again restoring this dual-pronged outreach. He has reestablished the "ministry of Peter" to the circumcision, the Jewish people.

Paul's Example

Throughout his ministry, the apostle Paul clearly took Yeshua's mandate seriously. Although called to be the apostle to the Gentiles, he always reached out to the Lost Sheep of the House of Israel first (see Matthew 10:6).

Consider Paul's commitment to this mandate:

> When they had passed through Amphipolis and Apollonia, they came to Thessalonica, where there was a Jewish synagogue. As his custom was, Paul went into the synagogue, and on three Sabbath days he reasoned with them from the Scriptures, explaining and proving that the Christ had to suffer and rise from the dead.
>
> Acts 17:1–3

Paul did the same thing in Salamis (see Acts 13:5), Antioch (13:14), Iconium (14:1) and Berea (17:10). Paul not only wrote that the Gospel was *to the Jew first*, but he also lived it out on his missionary journeys.

Origins of Anti-Semitism

Unfortunately, over the centuries this mandate to take the Gospel to the Jew first disappeared. If this was the example set by Paul, how then did so many Church leaders come to believe that God was finished with the Jews? If this were in fact true and God had finally had enough with Israel and cut them off, how could any of us trust in God's faithfulness toward us? At what point might He finally say enough with us and cut us off?

The change did not happen quickly.

Very early in the history of the Church, anti-Jewish sentiments began to appear. In fact, although they gave us momentous biblical truths, some of the great Church fathers missed it when it came to Israel and the Jewish people.

Origen (185–254), an early Church leader and theologian from Alexandria, began to teach that all biblical prophecies related to Israel were spiritual in nature and thus not to be taken literally. According to Origen there was no special place for the Jewish people in the fulfillment of God's plan on earth. The mantle had been passed to the Church. The Jews had become irrelevant.

The Church rejected Origen's teachings and branded him a heretic. He was excommunicated—twice. But his teaching would not go away. By the Council of Nicea in 325 it had taken root. In his book *The Church and the Jews: The Biblical Relationship*, Daniel Gruber writes:

> The anti-Israel spirit of this meeting can be seen in some of the statements of the council: "Let us then have nothing in common

with the most hostile rabble of the Jews. . . . In pursuing this course with a unanimous consent, let us withdraw ourselves . . . from that most odious fellowship [the Jews]" . . . There is no doubt that this council was an important turning point in the history of the Church. Israel was cast aside and the Church officially became the "new Israel."[1]

It became heretical for Jewish believers to observe the Jewish Sabbath and celebrate the feasts within the Church. "Good Christians" were prohibited from having any connection with the Jewish roots of their faith. The final nail had been driven into the coffin that laid to rest the Jewish heritage of Christianity.

With this action the idea of deicide was born—the accusation that the Jews were responsible for "killing the Son of God" and God would have nothing more to do with them. With the Church's decision to place responsibility for the death of Jesus squarely on the Jewish people, we see the predominant basis for anti-Semitism within the Church and the emerging doctrine of Replacement Theology.

You may be thinking the same thing I am right now—that those who were responsible for this were not true Christians. You need to understand, however, that most Jews do not know the difference between those who have a real relationship with Jesus and those who have merely identified themselves as Christians over the centuries.

Replacement Theology

As I mentioned briefly in chapter 2, Replacement Theology is the teaching that the Church has supplanted Israel as the apple of God's eye—that God's promises to the Jews no longer apply to the physical descendants of Abraham, but rather to His spiritual descendants. According to this way of thinking, the

Jewish people have no special place in God's plans, so there is no reason to make any special effort to reach them with the Gospel.

Replacement Theology became especially prominent in the fifth century when St. Augustine (AD 354–430) wrote in his book *The City of God* that the Christian Church had replaced the Jews as God's chosen people. In fact, Augustine considered unbelieving Jews to be the enemy of God's people. His teaching opened the door to more than fifteen hundred years of Jewish persecution at the hands of so-called Christians.[2]

It is difficult for me to understand how so many Christians can think that God has turned His back on all the promises He made to the descendants of Abraham, Isaac and Jacob. God means what He says, and He does not change His mind.

It saddens me and I believe it saddens the heart of God to see how little the Church-at-large participates in outreach to the Jewish people. If you compare the amount of time and money spent on reaching the Jewish people versus the various people groups in Africa, South America or Asia, you can see that Jewish outreach is a low priority for most Christians. In fact, for many Christians, it has zero priority.

It makes sense to me that even if a Christian believed it was no longer imperative to take the Gospel to the Jew *first*, he or she would still want to make an effort to reach out to the Jewish people as much as to any other people group. But that has not been the case.

Dual Covenant Theology

Another reason many Christians who love Israel do not reach out to the Jewish people with the Gospel is the negative influence of Dual Covenant Theology. At the absolute opposite end of the spectrum from Replacement Theology, Dual Covenant

Theology has the same end result—it withholds the Gospel from being shared with the Jewish people.

To put it as simply as possible, Dual Covenant Theology teaches that the Jewish people have a separate path to salvation through the Abrahamic or Mosaic Covenant. Proponents of this theology believe that faith in Yeshua is not necessary for Jewish people to obtain salvation. It teaches that both Judaism and Christianity are valid religions equally worthy of the other's full acceptance and respect. In other words, Christians ought not to challenge Judaism's rejection of Jesus as the Messiah. This well-intentioned yet false teaching emerged out of Christian guilt following the horrors of the Holocaust. In the wake of this tragic event in the history of so-called Jewish-Christian relations, liberal scholars began to teach that the Jewish people had suffered enough and should now be left alone. Again, although perhaps well intentioned, this teaching has helped create a mind-set, even among evangelicals, that Jews should be excluded from any efforts to share our faith.

Most Jewish people believe that Christians perpetrated the horrors of the Holocaust upon them. After all, the Nazi uniform featured a cross—albeit a twisted one. The Nazis claimed to be good Christians, and many of them truly believed what they were doing was in fulfillment of God's plan.

In addition to believing that the Jews were an inferior race, the Nazis believed the Jews had rejected the Son of God, were guilty of deicide (killing the Son of God) and now were God's archenemy. *Jew-ridden* was the philosophy that all Jews were to be exterminated from the earth. Of course, this is twisted thinking, but for many Jewish people, Christians were responsible for this horrific massacre in the name of their God, Jesus Christ.

My friend Rose Price, a Holocaust survivor and now a Messianic Jew, lost her entire family, except for one sister, in

Auschwitz. She related to me that the guards told her, "We kill you because you killed our God, Jesus Christ."

What began in Jewish-Christian relations as an attempt to convert the Jews to Christianity and later became forced conversion by the edge of the sword had now reached its climax: to destroy the Jewish people. The progression has been described like this:

> First it was, "Because you are Jews, you have no right to live among us as Jews."
>
> Next, it was, "Because you are Jews, you have no right to live among us."
>
> Finally, it was, "Because you are Jews, you have no right to live."[3]

For Christian scholars, it was clear that this suffering had been caused by the Church's efforts to force the Jewish people to convert to Christianity, and after the horrors of the Holocaust, it was now time to stop these conversion efforts and validate Judaism as a co-equal religion alongside Christianity. Sadly, this has resulted in the mind-set that any efforts to share Jesus with a Jewish person are distasteful and somehow socially incorrect.

Over time Dual Covenant Theology has made its way into the Bible-believing Church world. Today many Christians believe that they are *not* to share the Gospel with Jewish people.

It is a sad fact to recount, but many well-meaning Christians tried to share the Gospel with me as a teenager. When I responded that I was Jewish, every single one of them apologized. Quite unintentionally they were supporting my erroneous belief that Jesus was not for me as a Jew. And as I share in churches throughout the world I find that this remains a widely held view.

One Plan of Salvation for All People

I want there to be no misunderstanding: The Bible declares that there is only one plan of salvation for *all people*. "Salvation is found in no one else, for there is no other name under heaven given to men by which we must be saved" (Acts 4:12). Yeshua Himself said, "I am the Way and the Truth and the Life. No one comes to the Father except through me" (John 14:6, emphasis added).

As believers in the authority of the Bible, we have no choice but to accept this at face value. Either we believe God's Word or we do not. Either we believe that Yeshua died for the sins of all or we do not. There is no in-between. And there is no second Gospel for the Jewish people apart from a relationship with Yeshua. There is no provision for personal salvation contained in the Mosaic Covenant. It simply pointed to a New Covenant that was promised for a future time.

Spiritual Blindness

So why would born-again, Spirit-filled Christians miss this? Very simply, these erroneous Bible interpretations form blind spots for Christians.

Just as the Jewish people have been blinded with regard to the recognition of Yeshua as Messiah, the eyes of Christians also have been blinded from seeing the primary or foundational role that Israel plays in both the First Coming and the return of the Messiah to this earth, as well as the redemption of mankind.

At the root of Christian rejection of the Jewish people is the random spiritualization of Scripture—the theory, for example, that Israel no longer means the physical descendants of Abraham, Isaac and Jacob, but now refers to the Church. This is a dangerous approach to Scripture. In fact, this approach can negate the fundamentals of the faith, including the bodily resurrection of Messiah and His physical return to earth. It is one of the great blind spots that many Christians have when they look at Scripture.

As German evangelist Ludwig Schneider wrote, "Christians note the veil over the eyes of Jews that blinds them from seeing the Messiah, but when non-Jews do not believe that God's promises to Israel are still valid today, there is a veil over their hearts that encompasses all the nations."[4]

Heeding the Call

At Jewish Voice Ministries International, we take Paul's model seriously. We reach out to *all* people throughout the nations of the world, but we always go to the Jew first.

Our ministry is now bringing medical, dental and eye clinics to remote parts of the world such as Ethiopia and India. In these clinics we help thousands of non-Jews and share the Gospel with them. In fact we reach more Gentiles than Jews, but our motivation in going to these remote places is to reach out first to the Jewish communities.

Over the years I have spoken at numerous missions conferences that display huge banners declaring Romans 1:16, "I am not ashamed of the Gospel, because it is the power of God for the salvation of everyone who believes. . . ." In addition, I recently had dinner at a small diner on my way to Los Angeles where a large Christian motorcycle gang was eating. On the backs of their leather jackets was a large patch that quoted Romans 1:16, "The Gospel is the power of God for salvation to everyone who believes. . . ."

In both cases, the rest of the text is missing, " . . . first to the Jew, then to the Gentile." We must not forget that Romans 1:16, one of the great biblical principles of the New Testament, tells us that this Gospel is not only to the Jew as well as to the Gentile, *but it is to the Jew first*. It is the same Gospel—the same power of God—and it must be proclaimed to the Jew first if we are to do it in the biblical way. God is calling us to reach out to the

Jewish people with the one message of salvation through His Messiah, Yeshua.

I want to nip something in the bud right now. You may be thinking, *Well, God does not love Jews more than anyone else.* And you are absolutely right! God loves us all equally. "God so loved the world," we are told in the most famous verse of Scripture, John 3:16, "that he gave his only begotten Son that whoever believes in him would not perish but have everlasting life."

But this is not an issue of God loving one people more than another. It is an issue of divine priority. The Gospel began with the Jewish people. The promise of the New Covenant, written in Jeremiah 31:31–34 was *to* and *through* the descendants of Abraham, Isaac and Jacob.

God has remained faithful to that priority. It is not about a priority based on loving one people more than another, but on God's divine order. This is exactly what Paul is trying to communicate in Romans 11:15 when he writes, "What will their acceptance be but life from the dead?" There is a spiritual connection between the Gospel being proclaimed to the Jews and God's power being poured out—and then bringing the Gospel to the nations. Just as their rejection brought the Gospel to the other nations of the world, their restoration will bring about worldwide revival for the nations.

How Shall They Hear?

You may wonder how I can say that the Jewish people are open to the Gospel. Perhaps you have tried sharing with a Jewish person and felt as though you were talking to a brick wall. Even worse, you may have shared with a Jewish person only to be ridiculed. Or perhaps, like some Christians, you are reluctant to share your faith with Jewish people because you are under the erroneous belief that all Jewish people know the Bible better than you. Trust me, as a Jew brought up in a traditional Jewish home—and typical of 90 percent of the Jewish people here in America—this is simply not the case.

Yes, I went to synagogue growing up. Yes, I went to religious training every week. Yes, I learned to read Hebrew, but I never learned what the Hebrew meant. I could read Hebrew, but I could not translate it. Although we are called the People of the Book, the only real study I had of the Scriptures was in preparation for my bar mitzvah—a Jewish ritual rite of passage to signify a thirteen-year-old boy's traditional entry into adulthood. I was required to read a Torah portion in Hebrew from memory, along with the Hebrew prayers. I memorized what I was required to say. Other than that, I never learned what the Bible taught.

In reality, Jewish people overall have not rejected the Gospel—they have simply not heard the Gospel in a way that they can understand it. For you as a Christian, when you hear *Jesus Christ*, you hear "my Lord and Savior," but a Jew hears "God of Christianity." When you think of Church, you think of the people of God, true believers in Jesus the Messiah. But when Jewish people hear *Church*, they think, *Them*—the Gentiles, the people of the other religion. When we say *baptism* we think of a biblical mandate to enter into the death and resurrection of Yeshua. A Jew hears "leaving Judaism and converting to Christianity."

Likewise, the word *conversion* may bring to mind the biblical definition—repenting and turning to God—but Jewish people understand conversion very differently. For them, conversion means they are being asked to abandon their heritage and convert to another religion. For Jews, this is simply not possible, for we are taught that we are born Jews and we will die as Jews. This is rooted in our psyche. So Jewish people have not rejected Yeshua. Rather, they simply have not heard a Gospel that they can comprehend as valid for them as Jews.

Paul addresses this dilemma in Romans when he says essentially that it is easy to reach the Jewish people with the Gospel. In fact, Paul tells us in Romans 11 that it is easier for God to graft in the natural branches (the Jewish people) than it is to graft in unnatural branches (Gentiles). The challenge is that in order for them to believe, they need to hear.

> How can they call on someone if they haven't trusted in him? And how can they trust in someone if they haven't heard about him? And how can they hear about someone if no one is proclaiming him? And how can people proclaim him unless God sends them?—as the Tanakh puts it, "How beautiful are the feet of those announcing good news about good things!"
>
> Romans 10:14–15, CJB

A few verses later, Paul reemphasizes this truth with the familiar declaration: "So then faith comes by hearing, and hearing by the word of God" (Romans 10:17, NKJV). In context this verse refers to the restoration of the Jewish people. Paul specifically addresses the issue of Israel and their future in Romans 9, 10 and 11. Here, God makes it clear that He is not finished with the Jewish people, that He remains faithful to them and that in order for them to find true restoration and salvation, they must embrace the Gospel by faith. How do they receive that faith? Through our *proclamation* of the Word of God.

Because of Dual Covenant Theology, many well-intentioned Christians who love the Jewish people have been misled to believe that the Jewish people do not need a proclamation of the Gospel in order to come to faith. In addition, some believe that the salvation of Israel is for a future time and the work is to be done by a select group of evangelists. "It does not concern me," I have heard some say, "because it takes place after the Rapture, and Israel's time is yet for the future." Others have taught that unlike Gentiles, the Jewish people come to faith not by proclamation, but through revelation. In other words, although they need Jesus, He is revealed solely through supernatural acts of revelation rather than through hearing the Gospel proclaimed to them.

I know that all these are well-intentioned and that people who teach them love the Jewish people, but they are loving the Jewish people to death. This teaching is simply not biblical. Paul makes it clear that it is not revelation as opposed to proclamation, but that the revelation actually comes through the proclamation. That is the emphasis of the passage I just quoted.

In the outreaches I have conducted in the former Soviet Union since 1993, I have seen tens of thousands of Jewish people come forward in altar calls *in response to the Gospel*. Let me note again that they came in response to the proclamation of the Gospel just as Paul taught.

Proclaim!

How do they believe? They believe by hearing the Word of God! That Word must come to them from someone, and that someone is you!

It is misguided at best to avoid sharing the Gospel with Jewish people because you love them and do not want to offend them. Traveling to Israel and collecting Judaica, sending support to Israel or seeking to be Torah observant are no replacements for the mandate to provoke the Jewish people to jealousy and share your faith with that Jewish person whom God has placed in your life.

It would be far better to tell your Jewish friends, "I am a Bible-believing Christian and that means I am compelled to share the Gospel with all people. That means I cannot exclude you. But please know that my love for you is not dependent upon your response. My commitment to you as my friend is unconditional."

I am Jewish and I can tell you as a Jew that Jewish people will respect you for being honest and open and will be endeared to you for your expression of concern for them. They may not agree at first, but they will respect your view and your honesty.

I understand that it can be difficult to rock the boat and risk offending someone, especially when you know the person will not hesitate to respond defensively. I have been living this reality for over thirty years, and I know my own people well, but it is better to offend them than to avoid sharing your faith and not help to spare them from an eternity separated from their God.

I understand that you may be shy or feel as though you are unable to talk to your Jewish friends about Yeshua. Maybe you do not even know a Jewish person. At the very least, you can do two things: You can pray for the salvation of the Jewish people, and you can support ministries that are reaching out to them with the Gospel.

Israel Is Being Restored

God loves the Jewish people. He always has, and He always will. He made a commitment to Abraham, and He has remained faithful to that Covenant since the day He made it. He is committed to seeing Israel restored as a nation, both to their land and to their God. That day is coming . . . and has already begun!

God is the Father longing for His prodigal son, Israel, to return. Yeshua is like Joseph, waiting to embrace his other brothers, even though they did not recognize him and had mistreated him. He loves them, and that love is unconditional.

It is the heart of the Father to see every son and daughter of Abraham living happily in His Kingdom. He desires for all Abraham's children to come into their ultimate destiny, and that destiny is a relationship with Him.

But before Jesus can return to Jerusalem, the Gospel *must* be preached to every people group within every nation of the world, and it must be preached to the Jew first and then to the Gentile. We must follow Paul's model.

And as Yeshua draws ever nearer, they are listening as never before. As an eyewitness I can proclaim the wonderful testimony that God is fulfilling His Word. Israel is being restored. Jews are coming to faith in Yeshua in greater numbers than at any time since the first century. What does this mean for us?

It is just one more evidence that Messiah's return is at hand.

6

The Mystery of the Two Messiahs

*The fifth reason we can know
the last days are near:
The rise of Messianic expectation in Israel.*

You probably did not hear about the Messianic controversy that took place in Israel in 2007.

Although it caused quite a stir in Israel, for some reason it did not make much of a splash in America. It almost seemed like someone was trying to keep a lid on it. Strange, especially when you consider that our media feeds on controversy, and this one certainly should have been a ratings winner.

It started when Rabbi Yitzchak Kaduri died in Israel in February 2006. A highly regarded Sephardic rabbi born in Babylon, Kaduri was so popular that reports from some sources say 200,000 to 300,000 people came to his funeral. Kaduri was said to be around 108 years old at the time of his death.

About two years before he died, Rabbi Kaduri suddenly began warning his followers that the world was facing a series of terrible disasters. How did he know this? He said the Messiah had told him so. He declined to say where, when and how this conversation with the Messiah took place. All he would say was that he would reveal the Messiah's name when the time was right.

A rumor circulated that the old rabbi had written the Messiah's name on a small piece of paper, but that he also had requested the name not be read until one year after his death. According to *Israel Today*,[1] when the note was finally opened early in 2007, it contained a sentence of six words with the first letter of each word spelling out the Messiah's name: Yeshua.

The rabbi had also written, "Concerning the letter abbreviation of the Messiah's name, He will lift the people and prove that His word and law are valid. This I have signed in the month of mercy."[2]

Aviel Schneider, the newspaper reporter who broke the story about the rabbi's note, said he was urged not to publish the story. Schneider said he had never received so many e-mails, calls and other messages from people around the world—both negative and positive.

The rabbi's eighty-year-old son charged that the note was a forgery and said it was not written in his father's handwriting. In response, Schneider said that in preparation for his article, he had reviewed a number of the late rabbi's handwritten papers.

In addition, certain *symbols* had been drawn all over the pages. "They were crosses," the reporter said. "In the Jewish tradition, you do not use crosses. You do not even use plus signs because they might be mistaken for crosses. But there they were, painted in his own hand." Of course, Kaduri's family denied it, saying that the mysterious symbols were "signs of the angel."[3] You can just imagine the debate Schneider's story touched off within the Orthodox Jewish community in Israel.

Some leaders said that even if the note was authentic, the rabbi could not possibly have been talking about Jesus of Nazareth. That is because his revelation flies in the face of an almost two-thousand-year-old decision that Jesus was not the Messiah. They say Jesus did not fulfill the biblical prophecies about the Messiah found in the Tanakh (the Jewish Scriptures).

However, I am certain that the old rabbi had some type of encounter with the Messiah of Israel, Yeshua HaMashiach. He is not the only one. I know for a fact that a number of prominent rabbis in Israel have embraced Yeshua as Messiah but because of their position have remained secretive about their faith. I wish I could share more about this, but I can't.

Yet in general the leadership of mainstream rabbinic Judaism continues to hold fast to the position that Yeshua is not the Messiah, and nothing short of a visitation from heaven will convince them otherwise. In some cases, not even a divine visit would change their minds. In fact, the Talmud contains a reference that says if one hears a *Bat Kol* (a Hebrew term meaning "a voice from heaven") that runs contrary to the majority opinion of the rabbis, one should choose the opinion of the rabbis. In other words, the rabbis have the exclusive authority to interpret the Torah and continue its development. The sages of the Talmud carried this basic conception to an extreme but inevitable conclusion: "Even if they tell you that left is right and right is left, hearken unto their words until they tell you that right is right and left is left."[4] Although Jewish leaders for the most part agree that Jesus is not the Messiah, many ultra-orthodox Jews are heralding the soon coming of the Messiah. A May 2007 article in the Israel newspaper *Haaretz*, "Ex-chief Rabbi Opposes New Moves to Visit Temple Mount," reported that prominent rabbinic figure Zalman Melamed said, "Next year we will visit the Temple Mount together, with the ash of a red heifer, without arguments and without questions."[5]

The article illustrates the intense desire of some to see a rebuilt temple and sacrificial system, which they believe will usher in the coming of the Messiah.

The Jewish people are correct to be looking for the Messiah, but many of them do not yet realize that the Messiah they seek will be Yeshua, Jesus of Nazareth. The prophet Zechariah speaks of the day when they will recognize Him and be in a state of mourning when they realize that He is, in fact, Jesus (see Zechariah 12:10).

Christians and Messianic Jews, on the other hand, accept the claims of Yeshua because they understand that He did fulfill many of these prophecies. And those that He did not fulfill will be completed upon His Second Coming.

Why the difference? Are there two Messiahs? For religious Jews who are looking for the Messiah's coming the first time, two Messiahs are closer to the truth than we realize.

The Mystery of the Two Messiahs

We need to remember that Christians look at Messianic prophecy in hindsight through the lens of the New Testament. But for those who lived before Yeshua came and did not have the benefit of hindsight to illuminate these predictive prophecies, the idea of two Messiahs actually made a lot of sense. Why? Because when you look at all the Messianic prophecies together, there seems to be a contradiction.

Messianic prophecies can be divided into two distinct categories: a column A and a column B, if you will. Column A prophesies a suffering Servant, a gentle Healer, who will minister God's love to the poor and brokenhearted. This Messiah would be rejected, suffer and ultimately lay down His life for the sins of Israel. These prophecies focus on the love, mercy and forgiveness of God—the suffering servant Messiah. Since the

Middle Ages, Jewish scholars have tended to completely ignore these prophecies in order to counteract the growing threat and influence of Christian interpretation because they support the Christian claims that Jesus is the Messiah.

According to a story in the Talmud, a rabbi met the prophet Elijah and asked him, "When will the Messiah come?"

"Go and ask him yourself," Elijah replied.

"Where is he sitting?" the rabbi asked.

"At the entrance [the gates of the city]," came the reply.

"And by what sign may I recognize him?"

"He is sitting among the poor lepers."[6] This story clearly depicts the Messiah in column A.

Column B, on the other hand, prophesies a Messianic Age of world peace in which the Messiah will come as a warrior King who will take vengeance on God's enemies and rule and reign with justice, righteousness and divine order. It is to these prophecies that religious Jews point in order to reject Jesus as the Messiah, insisting that He neither fulfilled them nor ushered in an age of peace where the lamb and the lion lay down together, swords are beaten into plowshares and evil is destroyed forever (see Isaiah 2:4 and Micah 4:3).

Clearly, both types of prophecies *do* exist. The Jewish sages acknowledged that although contradictory, the prophecies were indeed speaking of the Messiah. They grappled with the apparent contradictions in an effort to reconcile them together, and eventually concluded that there must be two Messiahs.

To the first they gave the name Messiah ben-Joseph, or "Messiah, son of Joseph." Like Joseph, who was rejected by his brothers and eventually sold into slavery, this Messiah would also be rejected by His people. He would suffer and ultimately die.

They named the second one Messiah ben-David after King David. Like King David, who ruled during the Golden Age of Israel, this Messiah would come as King and reestablish Israel to her rightful place as head among the nations. He would establish peace in the world, and Israel would experience a Messianic Age of prosperity. According to this theory, Messiah ben-David would resurrect Messiah ben-Joseph, and they would rule and reign together.

In other words, two Messiahs would come at two different times. Together they would fulfill all the Messianic prophecies in the Tanakh.

What they failed to understand is that although these Messianic prophecies appeared to be contradictory, they referred to the same Messiah. Rather than two Messiahs each coming once, there would be one Messiah who would come at two different times. On His first visit to the earth Yeshua came as the sacrificial Lamb of God to take away the sins of the world (John 1:29). He will return, however, as the Lion of the Tribe of Judah in power to bring vengeance and justice. He will come as the conquering King leading a mighty army who will smite the enemies of God and destroy evil.

While the rabbinic theory of two Messiahs may seem far-fetched to many Christians, let me remind you again that we look back with the benefit of hindsight, which is 20/20. If you put yourself in the shoes of these ancient rabbis, you see that their theory was not so farfetched. They nearly had it right.

Yeshua Fulfilled Many Prophecies

Let's take a look at the prophecies Yeshua fulfilled the first time He came to earth. Yeshua:

- **was born** in Bethlehem (Micah 5:2).
- **was born** to a virgin (Genesis 3:15; Isaiah 7:14).
- **was called** out of Egypt (Hosea 11:1).
- **was rejected** by His own people (Isaiah 53:3).

- **is the Stone** the builders rejected, which then became the Capstone (Psalm 118:22–23).
- **is the gentle King** who entered Jerusalem riding on a donkey (Zechariah 9:9).
- **was betrayed** by a friend (Psalm 41:9).
- **was betrayed** for thirty pieces of silver (Zechariah 11:12–13).
- **was accused** by false witnesses (Psalm 35:11).
- **healed** the blind, deaf, lame and dumb (Isaiah 35:5–6).
- **bore our sicknesses** (Isaiah 53:4).
- **was spat upon,** smitten and scourged (Isaiah 50:6; 53:5).
- **was hated** without a cause (Psalm 35:19).
- **was pierced** for our transgressions and crushed for our iniquities (Isaiah 53:5; Zechariah 12:10; Psalm 22:16).
- **suffered** for the sins of many (Isaiah 53:10–12).
- **died** among criminals (Isaiah 53:12).
- **was put to death** but not because of His own transgressions (Isaiah 53:5; Daniel 9:26).
- **died** before the destruction of the Second Temple (Daniel 9:24–27).
- **had His garments divided** among those who cast lots for them (Psalm 22:18).
- **was buried** with the rich (Isaiah 53:9).
- **was resurrected** from the dead (Psalm 16:10–11; 49:15).

This is only a sampling. In fact, Yeshua fulfilled more than three hundred prophecies found in the Old Testament. One mathematician figured out that the odds of one man fulfilling only sixty of these prophecies would be one out of ten to the 895th power. Author Josh McDowell cites the odds of Jesus fulfilling only eight of the Messianic prophecies as one out of ten[17] (a one followed by seventeen zeros).[7] To put this into perspective, it is like covering the entire state of Texas with silver dollars two feet deep, marking one of them and having a blindfolded person pick the marked one, at random, the very first time he tries.

Not only did Yeshua fulfill Messianic prophecies found in the Old Testament, but other ancient writings also contain statements about His life and atoning death, including the Babylonian Talmud and the book of Josephus, to mention just two. The famous historian Josephus wrote this amazing statement about Yeshua:

> Now, there was about this time, Jesus, a wise man, if it be lawful to call him a man, for he was a doer of wonderful works—a teacher of such men as receive the truth with pleasure. He drew over to him both many of the Jews, and many of the Gentiles. He was [the] Christ; and when Pilate, at the suggestion of the principal men amongst us, had condemned him to the cross [AD 33, April 3], those that loved him at the first did not forsake him; and the tribe of Christians, so named from him, are not extinct at this day.[8]

Prophecies Still to Be Fulfilled

Jesus clearly fulfills the ancient prophecies that depict the Messiah as the servant who is rejected and suffers for the sake of His people. Yet Jesus's First Coming to earth did not fulfill other ancient prophecies, and for this reason many Jews reject Him as Messiah. Among those as-yet unfulfilled prophecies: He did not bring world peace (see Isaiah 2:1–4). The entire world did not acknowledge God as the one true God (see Zechariah 14:9). We do not live in a world in which the leopard lies down with the goat and the calf, lion and yearling live together in peace (see Isaiah 11:6–7). The lion does not eat straw like an ox (see Isaiah 65:25). Jesus did not destroy Israel's enemies (see Isaiah 29:4–6 and Isaiah 42:13).

Other prophecies found in Isaiah, Joel and Micah depict the returning King, prophecies that clearly remain to be fulfilled:

> He will strike the earth with the rod of his mouth; with the breath of his lips he will slay the wicked. . . . The wolf will live with the lamb, the leopard will lie down with the goat, the calf and the lion and the yearling together; and a little child will lead them. The cow will feed with the bear, their young will lie down together, and the lion will eat straw like the ox. The infant will play near the hole of the cobra, and the young child put his hand into the viper's nest. They will neither harm nor destroy on all my holy mountain, for the earth will be full of the knowledge of the LORD as the waters cover the sea.
>
> Isaiah 11:4–9

> The law will go out from Zion, the word of the LORD from Jerusalem. He will judge between many peoples and will settle disputes for strong nations far and wide. They will beat their swords into plowshares and their spears into pruning hooks. Nation will not take up sword against nation, nor will they train for war anymore.
>
> Micah 4:2–3

These are just a couple of the key Messianic prophecies that rabbis use to deny the Messiahship of Jesus. Yet a simple explanation lies in the New Testament truth that these are not separate Messiahs, but in fact, one Messiah who must return in order to fulfill these prophecies and finally accomplish God's ultimate plan for the redemption of the world.

A Brief History of Three False Messiahs

Many other men have either claimed to be the Messiah or have been proclaimed Messiah by their followers, but all have failed miserably. One of these men was Simon ben Kosiba (more commonly known as Simon bar Kokhba), who led a revolt against Rome in the second century. (*Ben Kosiba* means "Son of the Star," which his followers used in reference to Numbers 24:17: "A star will come out of Jacob; a scepter will rise out of Israel.")

Although bar Kokhba was certainly a charismatic leader, it was only after the revered Rabbi Akiva declared him to be the Messiah that he came to be viewed as Israel's redeemer. Sadly, his revolt was short-lived and came to a brutal end. According to Jewish historians, some leading members of the Sanhedrin were burned alive wrapped in Torah scrolls.[9] The famous Roman consul and noted historian Cassius Dio published a history of Rome in eighty volumes, reporting that more than 580,000 people were killed during the bar Kokhba revolt. It is impossible to know how accurate that number is, although archaeologists have found mass graves at several locations throughout the city.

Akiva's declaration of bar Kokhba as the Messiah caused the final split between the Jewish community and the Messianic Jewish followers of Yeshua. Because the Messianic Jews already knew Jesus was the Messiah, they refused to accept bar Kokhba as Messiah and did not join in this revolt. As a result, most of the Messianic Jewish community was spared from slaughter.

Another who claimed to be Messiah was Shabbethai Tzvi, who lived in the seventeenth century. Born in Smyrna of Spanish descent, Shabbethai was destined by his father to be a Talmudist. He spent his early youth in a *yeshivah* (Talmudic school) under the veteran rabbi of Smyrna, Joseph Escapa, but Tzvi showed no proficiency for the Talmud. Rather, mysticism and the Cabala (a body of mystical teachings of rabbinical origin, often based on an esoteric interpretation of the Scriptures) fascinated him. These involved asceticism and mortification of the body, including frequent bathing in the sea in winter, fasting for days at a time and living in a constant state of ecstasy. His devotees claimed these practices contributed to their ability to communicate directly with God and the angels, predict the future and perform miracles.[10]

At the height of his popularity Shabbethai had thousands of followers. He openly proclaimed himself as Messiah and wrote a letter, which said in part:

> The first-begotten Son of God, Shabbethai Tzvi, Messiah and Redeemer of the people of Israel, to all the sons of Israel, Peace! Since ye have been deemed worthy to behold the great day and the fulfillment of God's word by the Prophets . . . rejoice with song and melody, and change the day formerly spent in sadness and sorrow into a day of jubilee, because I have appeared.[11]

His followers were disillusioned when, faced with the threat of imprisonment or death, their would-be Messiah chose to convert to Islam. He wrote to them, "God has made me an Ishmaelite; He commanded, and it was done." He attempted to walk a tightrope between both faiths for a while, telling the Muslims that he was only maintaining contact with Jews because he wanted to convert them, and telling the Jews that he was only pretending to be a Muslim so that he might bring them to Judaism. Both groups eventually grew tired of him, and before long he vanished into obscurity.

The most recent of the false Messiahs was the late Rabbi Menachem Schneerson (1902–1994), leader of the Chabad-Lubavitch movement in Brooklyn Heights, New York. Although the rabbi himself never overtly claimed to be the Messiah, many of his followers clearly thought this was the case (some still do) and proclaimed him as Messiah.[12] After he died in 1994 they expected that he would rise from the dead. He was not the Messiah, and they are still waiting.

Why Did They Not Recognize Yeshua?

Why is it that so many Jews did not recognize Jesus when He came? At the time of Jesus, the Jewish people were subjugated under the rule of mighty Rome. They were looking for a Messiah who would deliver them from Rome's tyranny—One who would free them and reestablish Israel to the great prominence it had enjoyed under the united kingdom of King David.

It is not surprising that during this time period the Jewish people had such an expectation. Even Jesus's own disciples thought this was the case, which explains why they argued over which of them would be greatest (see Luke 9:45–48) and why the mother of James and John came to Yeshua and asked Him to give her sons places of authority in His Kingdom (see Matthew 20:20–24). It is also the reason why the last thing the disciples asked Jesus before His ascension was, "Lord, are you at this time going to restore the kingdom to Israel?" (Acts 1:6).

The majority of Jews today still do not recognize Jesus as the Jewish Messiah. Most Jews who believe in a literal Messiah are expecting a peacemaker who will restore the Jewish people to observances of Torah and bring supernatural peace and harmony to the world. Many Jews, however, have abandoned the idea of a literal Messiah altogether. Instead, they now refer to a "Messianic age," which is nothing more than a euphemism for an ultimate, utopian society that will one day be brought about through a commitment to social justice and helping the needy.

Yeshua Will Fulfill Every Biblical Prophecy

Let me be clear about one thing: Yeshua is going to return to earth, and when He does, *every single Messianic prophecy in the Old Testament* will come to pass. He will fulfill everything that the Bible says about Him in detail.

And His Second Coming will be nothing like the first. He has already come as the Lamb to take away our sins. He has granted the world two thousand years to repent and turn to Him. Now He will return as the Lion of Judah.

Revelation 19 describes it this way:

> I saw heaven standing open and there before me was a white horse, whose rider is called Faithful and True. With justice he judges and makes war. His eyes are like blazing fire, and on his head are many crowns. He has a name written on him that no one knows but he himself. He is dressed in a robe dipped in blood, and his name is the Word of God. The armies of heaven were following him, riding on white horses and dressed in fine linen, white and clean. Out of his mouth comes a sharp sword with which to strike down the nations. "He will rule them with an iron scepter." He treads the winepress of the fury of the wrath of God Almighty.
>
> Revelation 19:11–15

Many other prophecies relate to Messiah's return. Some are frightening in many ways because they relate to the raging fire of God's wrath and the destruction of His enemies.

I have heard some teach that the Jewish people will recognize Jesus as their Messiah and be saved only after He returns. And yet it is the First Coming that reveals the Lamb of God who takes away the sins of the world. It is the First Coming that demonstrates the mercy, forgiveness and redemption of a loving God. It is by knowing Him already that we are prepared to face the returning Messiah, the Lion of Judah. I do not see forgiveness and mercy at the moment of His return. I see a vengeful, angry lion with sharp teeth devouring everyone who dares to oppose Him.

For those who do not know the Lord upon His return, it will be a fearful thing to fall into the hands of a vengeful God. This is why we must proclaim the Gospel to all people—to the Jew first, according to the apostle Paul (see Romans 1:16). This is why Paul shares from the depths of his heart in Romans 9:1–4 his willingness to give up his very eternity for the sake of his own people, and why he implores the Church in Romans 10:1, "Brothers, my heart's desire and prayer to God for the Israelites is that they may be saved."

Now is the time to proclaim the Lamb of God that takes away the sins of the world. By the time He returns, it will be too late.

We Are in the Last of the Last Days

I am convinced from everything I see around me that we are in the final hour preceding the return of the Messiah to the earth. Israel and Jerusalem have been restored. God has been regathering His people both to the land and to Himself. The Gospel is being proclaimed throughout the nations of the world. The stage is being set, and we must be ready.

Prophecies concerning the last days describe terrible times ahead, and many certainly apply to the world we live in right now:

> There will be terrible times in the last days. People will be lovers of themselves, lovers of money, boastful, proud, abusive, disobedient to their parents, ungrateful, unholy, without love, unforgiving, slanderous, without self-control, brutal, not lovers of the good, treacherous, rash, conceited, lovers of pleasure rather than lovers of God—having a form of godliness but denying its power.
>
> 2 Timothy 3:1–5

> In the last days scoffers will come, scoffing and following their own evil desires. They will say, "Where is this 'coming' he

promised? Ever since our fathers died, everything goes on as it has since the beginning of creation."

2 Peter 3:3–4

Then you will be handed over to be persecuted and put to death, and you will be hated by all nations because of me. But he who stands firm to the end will be saved. And this Gospel of the Kingdom will be preached in the whole world as a testimony to all nations, and then the end will come.

Matthew 24:9; 13–14

Whether the Lord comes back tomorrow, next year or two hundred years from now really should not make any difference in the way we live. At the same time, the Lord wants His people to recognize the signs of the times and know that His return is at hand. We must be ready. *You* must be ready!

Growing expectation in the soon coming of the Messiah is visible throughout the observant Jewish community, not only in Israel but in America as well. Messianic excitement permeates the air. You can literally feel it. Everyone senses it. But what they do not yet see is that the Messiah they are longing for will turn out to be Yeshua. When He returns, He will fulfill all the remaining Messianic prophecies not yet completed. He will bring true and lasting peace to the earth. No, they do not see this yet . . . but they will. And it will happen soon.

7

Are "The Times of the Gentiles" at an End?

*The sixth reason we can know
the last days are upon us:
The times of the Gentiles are being fulfilled.*

They will fall by the sword and will be taken as prisoners to all the nations. Jerusalem will be trampled on by the Gentiles *until the times of the Gentiles are fulfilled.*

Luke 21:24, emphasis added

I love Jerusalem—there is no other city like it on earth. It is not only the capital of Israel, it is spiritually the capital of the world. Jerusalem is a majestic city that shines like gold as the sun rises in the morning and sets at twilight.

During Israel's golden age, Jerusalem was the capital of the great, undivided kingdom of David and Solomon. This was the place where the prophets and great heroes of the Bible worshiped the God of Israel. This is the city where Messiah taught, laid down His life for the sins of mankind and has resurrected, triumphing over death. And it is to this city that Yeshua will return. Indeed, dignitaries and people of all nations still today go there to seek Him.

Interestingly, Jerusalem is not situated in a strategically important location. Unlike places like Megiddo that control the *Via Maris* ("way of the sea"), the land bridge that connects the continents of Europe and Asia with Africa, Jerusalem has never had any real military value. The city is not on the ocean, so it has no ports, important for controlling sea trade routes. Yet Jerusalem has been one of the most sought-after land possessions in history. Over the centuries, Jerusalem has been conquered, rebuilt and conquered again. Like the phoenix, Jerusalem has arisen from the ashes after being destroyed time and time again—first by the Babylonians in 586 BC and again by the Romans in AD 70. After the Romans came the Arabs (sixth century), then the Crusaders (1099), then the Arabs again (fourteenth century), followed by the British (1917), who then gave it to King Abdulla of Jordan. Finally, in 1967 it came back under the control of the Jewish people after almost two thousand years.

Jerusalem is no doubt an important focal point of last days prophecy. This city, with a population of around six hundred thousand inhabitants, is small by world standards. Yet today, the land of Israel and, in particular, the city of Jerusalem are in the news almost daily. World attention has focused on this tiny nation and city. Why? What is all the fuss about?

It has to do with a very specific spiritual destiny that ties together God's purposes for a specific city with a specific people. In His sovereignty, He chose Jerusalem as the place to establish His Kingdom, reveal His glory and bring final deliverance and redemption to the world. The enemy understands this better than most of us, and so he has targeted his attacks there.

Not Important from a Human Perspective

From a human perspective, Jerusalem would not rank as one of the world's most important cities. She is not New York, Paris, London or Moscow. Even during the days when biblical history was being written in Jerusalem's streets, the city was not as significant as Alexandria, Rome or Athens. She has no strategic military importance, is not home to an important seaport (or a seaport at all), does not sit on an important trade route and has no significant natural resources, such as oil. Even so, oceans of blood have been shed over this city for the last three thousand years. And today, three thousand years after the reign of King David, a majority of the world's population still believes that Jerusalem is the most important city on earth.

There is only one possible reason for Jerusalem's importance: This city is important to God. Indeed, this is the city of the Great King.

Because Jerusalem is important to God and to His plans for the redemption of Israel and the nations, Satan has done everything within his power to keep Jerusalem out of Jewish hands and in a state of conflict. Archaeological digs reveal layer after layer of destruction as nation after nation has occupied this city and then been destroyed by the next conqueror. Yeshua spoke of this when He told His disciples, "Jerusalem will be trampled on by the Gentiles until the times of the Gentiles are fulfilled" (Luke 21:24).

A Brief History of Jerusalem

Jerusalem, the great capital under David and Solomon, was in its heyday a city of renowned splendor, highlighted by the magnificent Second Temple that had been built by Solomon and later enhanced by King Herod. It was one of the most beautiful structures of the ancient world. Jesus prophesied to His disciples regarding the Temple in Jerusalem: "As for what you see here, the time will come when not one stone will be left on another; every one of them will be thrown down" (Luke 21:6).

He was referring to the Roman destruction of the Temple in AD 70, an event that would take place approximately forty years later. In order to quell the continual uprisings led by the Zealots, a militant Jewish sect of the time, the Roman army stormed into Jerusalem under General Titus. The city was burned, and the Temple was destroyed and has never been rebuilt to this day. Hundreds of thousands of Jewish men, women and children were killed. The ruthless Roman Empire showed no mercy. They had decided to make the Jews an object lesson for any further acts of insurrection under their Empire.

Hundreds of prisoners were crucified in and around the city. Those who were spared were sent into exile. They were scattered throughout the Roman Empire—and eventually the entire world. Known as the Diaspora ("dispersion"), this event marked the final scattering of the Jewish people to the four corners of the earth, as God Himself had warned long ago.

> If you do not carefully follow all the words of this law, which are written in this book, and do not revere this glorious and awesome name—the LORD your God . . . you will be uprooted from the land. . . . Then the LORD will scatter you among all nations, from one end of the earth to the other.
>
> Deuteronomy 28:58, 63–64

Jerusalem became a broken-down shadow of its former glory. Josephus reported that "Jerusalem was so thoroughly razed to the ground by those that demolished it to its foundations, that nothing was left that could ever persuade visitors it had once been a place of habitation."[1]

The Roman Emperor Hadrian visited the ruins of Jerusalem in Judaea in AD 130 and decided to establish a pagan city-state on the Greek *polis* model with a shrine to Jupiter on the exact site of the former Jewish Temple. He renamed the city Aelia Capitolina after himself and Jupiter Capitolinus, the chief Roman deity.[2]

Only a few years later, as a result of the Bar Kokhba rebellion (AD 132–135), Hadrian decreed that no circumcised man should be allowed into Jerusalem and its territory or he would be killed. He forbade Torah study, Sabbath observance, meeting in synagogues and other ritual practices.[3]

Much of the Israeli countryside fell into desolation. The following information regarding the expulsion of all Jews from Israel by Rome's Emperor Hadrian and the "origins" of the name Palestine is not generally known among believers:

> As part of this policy of erasing the Jewish presence from Israel, Hadrian leveled Jerusalem and on top of the rubble rebuilt the pagan city he had planned, which he named Aelia Capitolina.
>
> . . . Whatever Jews remained in the area were . . . forbidden to enter Aelia Capitolina, [except on the] 9th of Av, so that they could be reminded of their greatest disaster and weep over the ruins of the Temple. . . . (A section of the Western Wall dubbed the "Wailing Wall" was the only part of the Temple that Jews could access for hundreds of years. This is where they came, wept and prayed.)
>
> For the first time since King David made it Israel's capital a thousand years earlier, Jerusalem was empty of Jews. It's ironic that the first city in history to be made intentionally and completely *Juden rein*, "Jew free" (to borrow a term later used by the Nazis), was their very own Jerusalem. . . .
>
> To further squelch any nationalistic feeling, Hadrian renamed the land Philistia (Palestine) after the Philistines, *an extinct people who . . . were some of the bitterest enemies of the Jews described in the Bible* [emphasis added].

This name survived in Christian writings, to be resurrected in 1917, after World War I, when the British took over the Middle East. . . . They named the lands east and west of the Jordan River . . . the Palestine Mandate. [F]rom this . . . the Arabs . . . get the name Palestinians. (Of course, at that time the Jews living in the Palestine Mandate were called Palestinians too.)[4]

Although some Jews always lived in the Middle East, it was not until 1844 that Jews began to return to Israel in any sizable numbers. The return of Jews to their historic homeland began as a trickle. By 1882, an estimated 24,000 Jews lived there. But at this time extreme persecution throughout Russia and Eastern Europe sent thousands of Jewish refugees fleeing in search of a safe haven, and the population of Israel continued to grow.

The Balfour Declaration

Following the defeat of the Ottoman Empire in 1917, control of the land then known as Palestine came under British control. Britain's then Foreign Minister Arthur Balfour was a committed Christian who believed that the return of Jews to Israel was connected to the Second Coming of Messiah. On November 2, 1917, the British issued what became known as the Balfour Declaration: "His Majesty's Government views with favour the establishment in Palestine of a national home for the Jewish people, and will use their best endeavours to facilitate the achievement of this object. . . ."[5]

Despite the declaration's call for "a national home for the Jewish people" in Palestine, nothing official took place. Encouraged by the rhetoric of the Balfour Declaration, however, a steady stream of Jews began to return to Israel.

Meanwhile, Arab residents of the region grew increasingly alarmed. The first recorded terrorist attack on an Israeli settlement occurred in 1920, when Arab villagers besieged Tel Hai, a Jewish settlement in Galilee near the Syrian border. Two months later, hundreds of Arabs descended on Tel Hai again, killing six more Jews. During the following months, armed Palestinian Arabs attacked more than a dozen Jewish agricultural settlements.

During the Passover and Easter holidays of 1920, Palestinian Arab pilgrims known as "Nebi Musa," on a pilgrimage to Jerusalem to visit what they believed was Moses' tomb, were incited to join in a violent plan to ransack the Jewish Quarter of the Old City of Jerusalem. The riot claimed the lives of five Jews and four Arabs and left 244 wounded—the vast majority of whom were Jewish. Sympathetic to the Arabs, the British military did not allow the Jews to arm themselves. This riot is considered to be the first act of terrorism launched by Arabs against the Jewish population in Israel.[6]

The Holocaust

The next significant event in history concerning the Jewish people was the rise of a madman named Adolf Hitler, who exterminated more than six million of the world's nearly eighteen million Jews in a span of just nine years. Two out of every three Jews living in Europe were wiped off the face of the earth. Even though this horrible act against the Jews caused sympathy toward the Jews in much of the world, including America, the British government, which still controlled the region known as Palestine, seemed to continue in a spirit of persecution against the Jews who sought to return to their homeland.

Due in part to pressure from Arab countries and Middle Eastern Muslims, Britain passed laws limiting the immigration of Jews to Palestine to only a few thousand a year. Ships filled with Jewish refugees were intercepted and forced to divert to

Cyprus. Thousands of Jews were placed in detention camps while the British government tried to figure out what to do with them. How ironic that some who had been liberated from Nazi death camps were again behind guard towers and barbed wire, this time imprisoned by the British! Jewish forces in Palestine under the leadership of the Irgun and Haganah forces then undertook a campaign to expel the British from the region.

Finally in 1947, the British agreed to withdraw, and the young United Nations voted in favor of a resolution to establish a Jewish homeland in Palestine. The land was partitioned into separate Jewish and Arab sections. The U.N. Partition Plan for Palestine, United Nations General Assembly Resolution #181, was a resolution adopted by the General Assembly of the United Nations on November 29, 1947.[7]

A Nation Is Reborn

In May 1948, the British withdrew and the State of Israel was proclaimed. The following day, Israel was invaded by five Arab states that surrounded it—Egypt, Jordan, Syria, Lebanon and Iraq. Surrounded by enemies who wanted to wipe them off the map, the tiny State of Israel was outnumbered sixty to one. Not only were the enemy armies much larger, but they also had vastly superior weapons and supplies.

The Arabs began attacking the newly formed nation. Yet the God of Israel—the God who neither slumbers nor sleeps (see Psalm 121:4)—kept Israel. Against all human odds the infant nation prevailed. With the establishment of the State of Israel, Jewish independence, lost two thousand years earlier, was renewed.

The new State of Israel was recognized immediately by the United States, the Soviet Union and Great Britain, and it was admitted as a voting member of the U.N. It may seem strange that the Soviet Union immediately recognized Israel, but even more baffling is that it also provided weapons. The founders of the State happened to be Russian immigrants who believed in Socialism, and Russia believed Israel would eventually become a socialist country and would accelerate the decline of British influence in the Middle East.[8] Thankfully, they were sorely mistaken.

Two Little-Known Facts Today

It is imperative to share with you a couple of facts that most people do not know:

First, it was the Arab nations and not Israel who refused to accept the partitioning of Palestine. Had they agreed to live in peace with their new neighbor, there would be a Palestinian state in the Middle East to this very day.

Second, the new Israeli government offered full citizenship to the Arab people within her borders. It has often been implied that Israel confiscated Arab lands and homes and drove people out of the country. In truth it was the Muslim countries who encouraged the Palestinian people (the Arabs living there) to leave Israel and then refused to take them in, leaving them struggling for survival in squalid refugee camps.

Why do I share this? Because I believe that Israel has an enemy, and that enemy is not flesh and blood. His name is Satan, and he is committed to the destruction of both this land and this people. The enemy has worked hard to turn world opinion against this tiny nation and people. As a result, most of the world's media has an extreme bias against Israel and promulgates a perpetual propaganda campaign that portrays Israel as the aggressor at every turn. I cannot say it any other way. This is nothing more than a lie from the pit of hell.

The Cold War and the Suez War of 1956

During the Cold War, which began in 1947, the Soviet Union poured billions of dollars in weapons into the hands of Israel's enemies. The Soviets encouraged the Arab nations to attack their tiny neighbor not once, but four times, and each time God gave Israel a decisive victory!

In the early 1950s, for example, Egypt closed the Suez Canal to Israeli ships. The United Nations ordered the canal open, but Egypt refused. Then, Egypt's President Gabel Abdel Nasser sent scores of terrorists into Israel, saying, "Egypt has decided to dispatch her heroes, the disciples of Pharaoh and the sons of Islam, and they will cleanse the land of Palestine. . . . There will be no peace on Israel's border because we demand vengeance, and vengeance is Israel's death."[9]

Nasser's foreign minister, Mammad Salah al-Din, added, "We shall not be satisfied except by the final obliteration of Israel from the map of the Middle East."[10]

This has been the Arab and Palestinian agenda since 1948 and remains their agenda to this day—the total annihilation of the State of Israel. The Arab nations and the Palestinians will not be satisfied until Israel is pushed into the sea.

Israel continued to demand that Egypt open the Suez Canal for Israeli shipping. Still the Egyptians refused. Hundreds of Israelis were killed as a result of these terrorist activities, and finally Israel had no choice but to retaliate. The Egyptian army was quickly and easily defeated, and Israeli troops pushed deep into Egyptian territory before a cease-fire was declared. President Eisenhower pressured the Israeli government to return the land that had been seized, and Israel complied.

The Six-Day War of 1967

In the first few months of 1967, information flooded into Israeli intelligence that the surrounding enemies were preparing for war. Then on May 20, Syria's Defense Minister Hafez Assad announced:

> Our forces are now entirely ready to . . . explode the Zionist presence in the Arab homeland. The Syrian army, with its finger on the trigger, is united. . . . I, as a military man, believe that the time has come to enter into a battle of annihilation.[11]

Ten days later, Israel's old enemy, President Nasser of Egypt, said:

> The armies of Egypt, Jordan, Syria and Lebanon are poised on the borders of Israel . . . while standing behind us are the armies of Iraq, Algeria, Kuwait, Sudan and the whole Arab nation. This act will astound the world. Today they will know that the Arabs are arranged for battle; the critical hour has arrived. We have reached the stage of serious action and not declarations.[12]

Finally, just days before the Arab nations of Egypt, Jordan and Syria, with contributions of troops and arms from Iraq, Saudi Arabia, Sudan, Tunisia, Morocco and Algeria, attacked tiny Israel, the Israeli military acted in a preventive strike. Within 24 hours, the Israeli Air Force almost completely destroyed the Egyptian Air Force. They then attacked the Syrian front on the Golan Heights and pushed Jordan back from the West Bank to the current borders that exist to this day. With this resounding victory, Israel had gained control of the Sinai Peninsula, the Gaza Strip, the West Bank, East Jerusalem and the Golan Heights. In an astounding display of force that took only six days, Israel completely crippled the combined armies of Lebanon, Syria, Jordan and Egypt.

The world was astounded. After six days of war, the Arab coalition was utterly defeated. The results of Israel's victory affect the geopolitics of the region to this day.[13]

This stunning defeat was nothing short of miraculous. In fact, I believe the handprint of God was all over this war. Countless stories of divine interventions that took place during this war have been described in detail. In his book *The Ghost of Hagar*, author George Otis Sr. described some supernatural events that actually occurred during the bombardment.

> This war was started on . . . our Sabbath. The Arabs were almost unstoppable because of the timing of their sneak attack, and from hitting on both the Suez and Golan fronts simultaneously, we obviously weren't quite ready. Further, they shook us terribly with the introduction of the new Russian Sagar wire-guided, anti-tank missiles. . . .
>
> At the worst point of the battle . . . there were only three Israeli tanks left to block the path of that terrible armored horde from rolling down into Tiberias. The Arabs had advanced all the way from Damascus, but somewhere in the Bible it says, "The Lord God of Israel fought for Israel" (Joshua 10). . . . Suddenly the Syrian General . . . issued an order over the command radio to his tanks and troops . . . : "The Israelis have almost entirely stopped firing. I don't like the feel of this situation at all. (He had no way of knowing that there were only three Israeli tanks still able to fire). I think the Israelis must be drawing us into a trap to ambush us. Stop immediately right where you are! I think we should stop for lunch and refueling!"
>
> That two-hour halt . . . gave us just enough time for sizable numbers of new tanks, troops, artillery and ammunition to reinforce our three remarkable Israeli tanks. The Syrian's "lunch break" was their high-water advance point. In days, the whole momentum of the battle shifted. I tell you, it was unexplainable, and I think it may have been the hand of God![14]

The most significant prophetic fulfillment to come out of the Six-Day War was the reestablishment of the Old City of Jerusalem under Jewish control. For the first time in more than two thousand years, the city and the Temple Mount were again controlled by the Jewish people—a direct fulfillment of Luke 21:24. This signaled a transition period in biblical history—a shift away from the time of the Gentiles back to Israel.

The Yom Kippur War of 1973

The next war began on Saturday, October 6, 1973. It was the Sabbath as well as Yom Kippur, the holiest day in the Jewish calendar. Israel was not prepared for the coordinated surprise attack undertaken by Egypt and Syria. In fact, Egyptian and Syrian military strategists believed that if they attacked Israel on the holiest day of the year, Israel would be unable to respond. How wrong they were! Nearly the entire Israeli army was worshiping in synagogues, so it was actually quite easy to locate and transport troops to the front. The Israeli Army simply sent trucks around to the various synagogues throughout the Israeli cities, and from there delivered the soldiers directly to the front. Still, the tiny nation was caught off guard.[15]

On the Golan Heights, less than 200 Israeli tanks faced an invasion of 1,400 tanks from Syria. Along the Suez Canal, some 436 Israeli soldiers were tasked with holding off an estimated 80,000 Egyptian troops.

At least nine Arab countries were actively engaged in the assault on Israel, contributing troops, weapons and/or money. The official ruler of Libya at the time, Muammar Gaddafi, sent one billion dollars in military aid to Egypt.

Thrown onto the defensive during the first two days of fighting, Israel mobilized its reserves and eventually repulsed the invaders and carried the war deep into Syria and Egypt. The Arab states were swiftly resupplied by sea and air from the Soviet Union, which rejected U.S. efforts to work toward an immediate cease-fire. As a result, the United States belatedly began its own airlift to Israel. Two weeks later, Egypt was saved from disastrous defeat by the U.N. Security Council, which had failed to act while the tide was in the Arabs' favor.[16]

The Israeli Plight

This has been the plight of Israelis since 1948. They are either at war or constantly being threatened by war. The daily rocket attacks from Gaza threaten this country at all times. We in America and Europe cannot fathom this reality. Although America experienced a quick taste of this on September 11, 2001, our state of high alert and anxiety lasted only a short period of time, and everything returned to the status quo.

Israel, however, does not have this luxury. Iran's President Mahmoud Ahmadinejad is constantly ranting and raving against Israel. He has declared openly that as soon as they accomplish their ambition of building a nuclear weapon, they will launch it against Israel without hesitation. In addition, Hezbollah forces in Lebanon have amassed a stockpile of weapons to use against Israel, pledging themselves to Israel's destruction, not to mention that Israeli citizens are constantly enduring attacks from Hamas, now based in Gaza, the land that Israel returned to the Palestinians in hopes of peace. Incidentally, the 1988 Hamas Charter, which they at one time promised to amend, continues to call for the destruction of Israel and its replacement with an Islamic state.

A once moderate Egypt is now under the control of the Islamic Muslim Brotherhood as a result of the Arab Spring and is on the verge of terminating the fragile peace treaty that has been in effect with Israel since Sadat was president in 1979. Syria and Jordan are in upheaval and may eventually be replaced with regimes that are more fanatic and less restrained in their hatred of Israel.

Although Israel has built one of the greatest armies in the world, her survival through the millennia, her reestablishment back to the land and her survival since declaring statehood in 1948 are nothing short of miracles of God. There simply is no explanation other than a faithful God who has promised that as long as the sun shines by day and the stars shine by night, Israel will continue to be preserved (see Jeremiah 31:35–37).

Please understand me correctly. I am not saying that the Arab or Muslim people are evil or *the enemy* in any way. God loves the Arab people every bit as much as He loves the Jews. Yeshua died for the entire world, and that includes both Jews and Arabs.

But He promised the land now known as Israel to the children of Abraham, Isaac and Jacob as an everlasting possession. He chose the children of Israel to be His holy nation. He promised to remain faithful to them to the end. God is not a man that He should lie (see Numbers 23:19), and He remains faithful to those promises.

But sadly the days of terror and violence are not yet over for the Jewish people. Satan continues to live under a death sentence (Genesis 3:15) that he refuses to accept. He will not go down without a fight. Just as he tried in ancient times to destroy the Jews and thwart God's plan through Pharaoh, Haman and Herod, in more recent years he has used people like Hitler, Nasser and Ahmadinejad to carry out his plans.

Satan is a wounded animal. And just as a wounded animal is even more hostile and dangerous, he is doing everything he can in a last-ditch effort to thwart God's plan. The attacks against Israel and the Jewish people will only continue to intensify as we move closer to the return of Jesus.

But I have good news! God is fulfilling His prophetic promise to restore Israel, and that signals the near return of Jesus the Messiah to the earth. Soon Satan will be put down for good. When he is, and Yeshua reigns on the earth, life on this planet will be nothing short of glorious.

Will the United States Turn against Israel?

Since becoming a nation in 1948, the United States has been Israel's closest ally. The United States has recognized that, as the only true democracy in the Middle East, this tiny nation is an important friend. Responsible for billions of dollars of financial aid, the U.S. has been the key provider of defensive weapons for the Israeli military. Although Richard Nixon's reputation in America is not the best, the former president remains a hero in Israel. Nixon provided critical weapons and supplies to Israel during the Yom Kippur War that helped turn the tide and ultimately secured an Israeli victory.

I have no doubt that America's support of Israel over these last 65 years has invoked the blessings of God. The promise to "bless those that bless Israel and curse those that curse Israel" in Genesis 12:3 is a divine decree that is just as true today as when it was written. History has borne out this fact.

Sadly, Zechariah prophesied the day when all the nations of the earth would turn their backs on Israel:

> I am going to make Jerusalem a cup that sends all the surrounding peoples reeling. Judah will be besieged, as well as Jerusalem. On that day when all the nations of the earth are gathered against [Israel], I will make Jerusalem an immovable rock for all the nations. And all who try to move it will injure themselves.
>
> Zechariah 12:2–3

If I understand these verses correctly, "all nations" turning against Israel will eventually include the United States. Indeed I fear the day that America fully turns her back on Israel, because that will be the beginning of the end for our beloved country. Sadly, our relationship with Israel has been strained in recent years as America continues to try to force Israel's hand to give up her God-given land in exchange for an empty peace. A two-state solution on the land that God gave as an eternal inheritance to the children of Abraham, Isaac and Jacob is not in keeping with God's will, and He is and will continue to speak up on the matter. It is likely that America will continue to exert more pressure on Israel, and ultimately the wonderful relationship that we have experienced for these past 65 years will dissolve. The recent declaration by President Obama that Israel needed to return to pre-1967 borders, which is indefensible given her demographic realities, was a significant step in that direction.

Thank God for the evangelical community that loves Israel and keeps praying and speaking out as watchmen on the walls. Israel now understands that evangelical Christians are Israel's best friend and can be relied on for support.

I encourage you to continue to pray regularly for God's peace plan for Israel and Jerusalem—a peace plan that is rooted in both Jew and Arab coming to know Yeshua (Jesus) as their Messiah and Lord. Only then can true peace between both peoples exist. This was and always has been God's peace plan, and it is the only way that lasting peace can come to this troubled land. I also encourage you to speak up and make your voice known to your government representatives and the White House. Other ways that you can bless Israel include taking a trip to Israel to show your support and partnering with ministries that seek to bring Israel the greatest blessing possible: a relationship with their Messiah.

The Times of the Gentiles Are Being Fulfilled in Our Day

"Jerusalem will be trampled on by the Gentiles until the times of the Gentiles are fulfilled" (Luke 21:24). This is exactly what has happened since Jesus gave this prophecy regarding the signs of the last days to His disciples almost two thousand years ago. Since then, Jerusalem has been conquered and re-conquered by the Romans, the Byzantines, the Arabs, the Crusaders, the Arabs again under the Ottoman Empire, the British and the Jordanians.

The establishment of the State of Israel in 1948 and the reconquering of the city of Jerusalem in 1967 are prophetic events that mark a transition in biblical history. They are the time clock for the last days, and the clock is now ticking. They also signal the near return of Jesus to the earth. As a result of the Six-Day War in 1967, the Jewish people regained control of Jerusalem. The return of the holy city into Jewish hands is a direct fulfillment of Yeshua's statement in Luke 21. The restoration of Jerusalem back to the Jewish people signaled the "until" of Luke 21:24 and marked a historic shift in biblical history, as this restoration is absolutely essential to Jesus' return to earth.

Until 1967, it was impossible for Jesus to return, since we are told in Matthew 23:39, "For I tell you, you will not see me again until you say, 'Blessed is he who comes in the name of the Lord.'" He was speaking of the Jewish inhabitants of Jerusalem. Only a Jerusalem under the control of the Jewish people would make it possible for this prophecy to be fulfilled. In other words, without a reestablished Israel under the control of the Jewish people, Jesus could not return. Yet the land and its capital city have been returned to them, meaning that the "times of the Gentiles" are at an end.

The stage, therefore, for His Second Coming is set.

A Spiritual Revival That Parallels the Physical One

Yeshua's prophecy in Luke that Jerusalem would be trodden down until the time of the Gentiles is fulfilled is directly connected to another Scripture that refers to the times of the Gentiles in relationship to Israel—Romans 11:25: "I do not desire, brethren, that you should be ignorant of this mystery, lest you should be wise in your own opinion, that blindness in part has happened to Israel until the fullness of the Gentiles has come in" (Romans 11:25, NKJV).

When we link these Scriptures together, we see a relationship between the land—Jerusalem—and the people—Israel. This is a key mystery that has been unfolding and is absolutely critical to understanding the last days. Back in chapter 4, I talked about the fact that Israel has been subject to a blindness that will continue until a set time in history referred to as "the fullness of the Gentiles" and that many Bible teachers mistakenly interpret *fullness* as "full number," as if some quota of Gentiles must first be saved before God will again save Jewish people.

I understand the Greek word *pleroma* differently and believe Paul here is talking about "fullness," not "full number." The fullness of the Gentiles coming in is the same event as the times of the Gentiles being fulfilled that Jesus referred to in Luke 21. They both mark a set period in divine history that God has ordained to restore both the land and the people of Israel. Immediately following the Six-Day War and reestablishment of Jerusalem into Jewish hands in 1967, the Spirit of God began to pour out on the Church and a revival sprang up. Historians label this the Jesus Movement. Others call it the Charismatic Renewal. A little-known fact is that during this period of 1967–1980, thousands of Jewish youth who were searching for greater meaning and purpose in their lives began to embrace Jesus and were saved. This is no coincidence. God's appointed time had arrived for Jerusalem to come back under Jewish control and for the blindness to begin to lift from the eyes of the Jewish people. Over 35 years later, this transition continues as more and more Jewish people can see who Jesus really was and is.

With this newfound faith and purpose, these young Jewish believers also began to reconnect with their Jewish heritage and upbringing. This eventually led to the establishment of the modern Messianic Jewish movement. From then on, this movement has continued to grow.

Gary Thoma, writing in *Christianity Today*, said:

> The rapid growth of Messianic Judaism has been remarkable. In 1967, before the Jewish people regained control of Jerusalem, there was not a single Messianic Jewish congregation in the world, and only several thousand Messianic Jews worldwide. Today, [more than] 350 Messianic Jewish congregations—50 in Israel alone—dot the globe. There are well over one million Jews in the United States who express some sort of faith in Yeshua.[17]

The Messianic Jewish movement certainly has flourished. Not only are such congregations in the United States and Israel, but Messianic congregations also are flourishing throughout Western Europe, the former Soviet Union and South America. In fact, Messianic Jewish congregations exist in almost every city of the world that has a significant Jewish population.

Right now, more Jews believe in Yeshua than at any other time in history. It is probable that more Jewish people have come to faith in Yeshua since the reestablishment of Jerusalem in 1967 than in any period of time in the past two thousand years. This clearly establishes a direct connection between Yeshua's words in Luke 21:24 and Paul's words in Romans 11:25. This direct correlation indicates that God's restoration of the Jewish people physically back to the land is connected to his restoration of them spiritually back to Himself through His Messiah.

The Time to Favor Zion Has Come

Israel and Jerusalem are back in Jewish hands. The people of Israel, who have been scattered throughout the world, are returning to their land, and perhaps most important, they are returning to their God. This is great news for the Church and something to which every true follower of Jesus should be paying attention. Indeed, we should be rejoicing, because this is a clear sign that we are in the last days and that Jesus is about to return. The sign of Israel's restoration means that both the Church and the world are about to experience the resurrection of life from the dead.

And every believer is to play a role in this prophetic shift. My prayer is that every believer will wake up, shake off complacency and realize the time is short. We need to be about our Father's business and do His work "as long as it is day . . . [for] Night is coming when no one can work" (John 9:4). Everyone reading this book has Jewish friends who need to hear the Gospel, and God is calling you to "provoke them to jealousy" (see Romans 11:11, NKJV). The spiritual restoration of the Jewish people is at hand!

We are living in ever-changing times. As the time of the Gentiles comes to a close, it is God's time to return to Israel—just as He promised. The time to favor Zion has come!

You will arise and have compassion on Zion, for it is time to show favor to her; the appointed time has come.

Psalm 102:13

PART TWO

YOUR ROLE IN USHERING IN GOD'S KINGDOM

8

Bringing "Life from the Dead"

Sammy Hellman has been my tour guide in Israel for more than 25 years. During that time, he has become a dear friend of mine. I do not know if he is a believer yet. Sometimes, by the way he answers my questions, I think he is. Other times I am not sure. But he is certainly open to Messianic thought, and when he guides Israel's tourists, they think he is a follower of Yeshua. He has more passion and love for the land of Israel than any person I have ever met.

Sammy fought in both the Six-Day War of 1967 and the Yom Kippur War of 1973, and on his guided tours he relives his experiences. Originally from Romania, Sammy survived the Nazi occupation of his country and moved to Israel with his parents immediately after the war ended. He is a strong man who has endured much hardship in both Romania and Israel.

There is a deeply spiritual side to Sammy, and he loves to attend our worship services. Yet he always seems more like an observer than a participant. Still I often notice as we worship that he has tears in his eyes.

Many years ago, something happened that made a tremendous impression on Sammy. I know the story in detail because I have heard it many times. He still says he does not know what to make of it. I can tell what a deep impact this experience had on Sammy because of the look that comes over his face as he tells the story. He often gets caught up in the emotion of it all. It happened when he was serving as a tour guide for a black Pentecostal group from the United States and went to pick up the group at their hotel in Jerusalem.

"Out of the corner of my eye," Sammy relates, "I saw this elderly, gray-haired woman stumble on the top step. Before anyone could help her, she tumbled all the way down a flight of ten or twelve concrete steps. She landed hard at the bottom and lay there motionless. It was a terrible fall. I knew she was badly injured."

Sammy ran to her side, picked up her arm and felt for a pulse. Nothing.

"She was dead," he says. "Beyond any shadow of a doubt. I fought in two wars and saw death with my own eyes. I know what death looks like, and she was dead."

The woman's pastor reached the dead woman next. The man bent down, began gently stroking her hair and quietly blessed and prayed for her, asking the Lord to heal her.

Then he spoke to her, "Get up, Mrs. Wilson. You are not supposed to leave us. You are not supposed to disappoint Jesus, because He brought you here. He was the One who wanted to share with you His homeland. Now, you are going to stand! Now, you are going to stand!"

Sammy says, "I remember clearly that he said it twice: 'You are going to stand!'"

Her arm twitched. Then she began to stir. Within a few minutes, she was sitting up and asking for someone to bring her purse, which she had dropped during her fall.

She insisted that she did not need to see a doctor. She was fine. She boarded the bus and spent the day touring Israel as planned.

Tears well up in Sammy's eyes when he remembers what he saw that day. "She was more than eighty years of age," he whispers. "I was sure she had passed away. There was no doubt about it. I was not 100 percent sure of this—I was 150 percent sure!" He shakes his head in wonder.

Like so many Jewish people I know, Sammy does not want to answer the question posed by Yeshua, "Who do *you* say that I am?"

In the third chapter of Acts, Peter calls upon the people of Israel to respond to the Good News of Messiah:

Repent, then, and turn to God, so that your sins may be wiped out, that times of refreshing may come from the Lord, and that he may send the Christ [Messiah], who has been appointed for you—even Jesus. He must remain in heaven until the time comes for God to restore everything.

Acts 3:19–21

It is clear to me that this passage of Scripture is related to what Paul says in Romans:

Inasmuch as I am the apostle to the Gentiles, I make much of my ministry in the hope that I may somehow arouse my own people to envy and save some of them. For if their rejection [of Jesus] is the reconciliation of the world, what will their acceptance be but life from the dead?

Romans 11:13–15

Notice that Paul says there is a connection between the rejection of Yeshua (Jesus) by Israel and the reconciliation of the world. If this reconciliation was the result of Israel's rejection, how much more wonderful is it going to be when they accept Him?

As openness to the Gospel began to diminish among the Jewish people toward the latter part of the first century, the doors of His Kingdom opened wide to the Gentile nations. This is clearly illustrated in Paul's missionary journeys. Paul always went to the synagogue first, and only when he was rejected from the synagogue did he go into the streets and testify to the Gentiles. Because of the Gentiles' easy acceptance of the Gospel message, the number of Gentiles quickly exceeded the number of Jewish believers.

The same link that caused the Gospel to go to the Gentiles upon the Jews' rejection exists with their acceptance. When the Jewish people return to their God, something even greater than the Gospel going to the nations will occur. Paul tells us it will bring life from the dead!

While there is debate as to whether this refers to a spiritual or physical awakening, one thing is clear: It is an important key in the return of Yeshua to this earth. I cannot overstate this parallel destiny between the Church and Israel. Scripture is clear that God's concern is the restoration of the world—of all mankind—but the key that unlocks this redemption is Israel. The redemption of Israel signals redemption for the world!

Israel and Japan

I spent a number of years traveling and lecturing in Japan. Why Japan? Because I was intrigued that even though only 1 percent of the Japanese profess faith in Jesus, most of those who do are members of the intelligentsia. They are doctors. They are professors and lawyers. And they have become fascinated with Israel.

They understand that the destiny of Japan is connected inseparably to the destiny of Israel. These people pray daily for the salvation of Israel, and they know that when it comes, it will directly affect their nation. It will bring *life from the dead* and *times of refreshing*.

The fact is, the destiny of all nations, including our own, is connected to the destiny of Israel. We are inseparably tied together, like it or not. If you want to understand the role that Israel and the Jewish people play in the return of the Messiah, understand that it is equal to or more important than their role in His First Coming.

Yeshua was born to Jewish parents in Israel, the Jewish homeland. His ministry was to the lost sheep of the house of Israel. His first disciples were all Jewish, and they took the Gospel to the nations. It is impossible to separate Yeshua from His Jewish identity and mission in the same way that it is impossible to separate His return from the role that Israel plays when they cry out, "Blessed is he who comes in the name of the Lord" (Matthew 23:39).

When I am in Japan, I tell people, "If you want to see Japan saved, pray for the salvation of Israel." When I am in India I say, "If you want to see India saved, pray for the salvation of Israel." Here at home in the United States, I tell people that if we want to see America turn to God in a very big way, we need to pray for the salvation of Israel.

The Wrap-up of God's Plan

I believe the salvation of the Jewish people will release the power of God, and a mighty worldwide revival will result—a revival far greater than any the world has ever seen. It will be the final fulfillment of the great outpouring spoken of by the prophet Joel:

> I will pour out my Spirit on all people. Your sons and daughters will prophesy, your old men will dream dreams, your young men

will see visions. Even on my servants, both men and women, I will pour out my Spirit in those days.

Joel 2:28–29

I believe that the fulfillment of this verse is Satan's greatest fear, and he is working around the clock to try to prevent it from happening. He knows that the end result of *life from the dead* will result in his death sentence being carried out as prophesied in Genesis 3:15. He understands that the only way to keep this from being fulfilled is the destruction of the Jewish people.

Some scholars believe that the *life from the dead* to which Paul refers in Romans 11 is a physical resurrection of the dead that will be connected to the return of the Messiah. Most say it is talking about a spiritual renewal. But I see something far greater than individual salvation in this revelation. I am convinced that *life from the dead* is related to the fall of Adam and the restoration of all things. It has to do with finishing the work of atonement that restores the earth to its pre-Adamic state.

Life from the dead is the termination of the curse of man's fall from grace once and for all. It is the eradication of sin, death and suffering, our final enemies. Stated differently, it is the "restoration of all things" that Peter spoke of in his powerful exhortation to his Jewish brethren in the Temple.

> Repent therefore and be converted, that your sins may be blotted out, so that times of refreshing may come from the presence of the Lord, and that He may send [the Messiah] Jesus Christ, who was preached to you before, *whom heaven must receive until the times of restoration of all things*, which God has spoken by the mouth of all His holy prophets since the world began.
>
> Acts 3:19–21, NKJV, emphasis added

I interpret "life from the dead" and "restoration of all things" as speaking of the same event; they are synonymous. It is the wrap-up of God's plan for planet earth ordained before the beginning of time.

Until that glorious day comes we will continue to live in a world tainted by the curse pronounced on Adam and Eve. Do not get me wrong. The Scriptures contain promises that I believe we can appropriate for health, healing and divine provision. We are new creations in the Messiah, and we can enjoy the benefits of what Jesus provided for us at Calvary. But we live in a fallen world and must endure the consequences of that condition. The evidence of this is all around us. A lawn or garden left to itself will soon be shaggy and overgrown with weeds. You can stand over your garden and pray that the weeds will go away, but until the curse is ended, it is probably wise to spray them with weed killer or pull them.

No matter how much we pray, we still age, and our hair still falls out. Bad things still happen. Murderous military regimes, dictators and evil leaders remain at large in the world. Genocide still plagues us in places such as Darfur, Sudan, Bosnia, Rwanda, Cambodia, Africa and Burma.

But when Yeshua returns all this will change! When life comes from death, we will be living in a world that operates as it was originally intended. It will be a return to the Garden of Eden.

A World without Death

Imagine turning on the evening news or opening your morning paper and seeing nothing depressing or upsetting. Imagine no drive-by shootings, no fatal auto accidents, no suicide bombings, no global food crises, no starving children anywhere in the world, no oil spills, no devastating tsunamis and no earthquakes. How about no more terrorist attacks or threats of nuclear weapons. It will be wonderful to live in a world like that!

The good news is that this world is on its way. The better news is that you can help speed up its arrival. How? By doing your part to reach the Jewish people with the Gospel. You can share Yeshua with the Jewish people among your acquaintances. You can pray for the Jewish people around the world to come to the saving knowledge of their Messiah. This is the key that will ultimately result in *life coming from the dead*.

I believe the understanding of what Israel's restoration would mean for the redemption of the nations was one of the reasons Paul was able to say, "For I could wish that I myself were cursed and cut off from [Messiah] Christ for the sake of my brothers, those of my own race, the people of Israel" (Romans 9:3–4). Paul was writing to the Gentiles and sharing his burden not for them but for his own brethren, the Jews. It seems more likely that he would have told the Gentiles he would sacrifice his personal salvation for them. It would have made more sense, in a way, if he had said, "I have a continual sorrow in my heart for you in Rome, for I would be willing to give up my salvation that some of you might be saved." But he did not do that. By telling a Gentile audience that his greatest burden was not for them but for his Jewish brethren, he risked offending many of them. Yet Paul took the risk because he understood that the salvation of their countrymen was tied to the salvation of the Jewish people.

He understood that the end result of their coming to Yeshua would bring about the return of the Messiah. In other words, Paul was willing to give up his salvation to see God's ultimate plan for the world accomplished, and that plan first required the salvation of his Jewish brethren. Paul shared this with the hope that those who love him would share his burden with him. He was enlisting their prayer, love and support to bring about their salvation, which in turn would bring about the salvation of their own families.

We must heed Paul's words. They are just as true today as they were when he wrote to the church at Rome almost two thousand years ago. God's plan remains the same. The revival of Israel is tied to revival for the world; the restoration of the Jewish people is inexorably tied to the restoration of all mankind.

Time to Be Co-workers

Now is the time to be co-workers with the Holy Spirit in hastening Yeshua's return by taking the Gospel to the Jewish people all over the world. Perhaps you have no Jewish people in your life. Pray and God will bring them. Perhaps you do not live in an area where Jewish people live. The very least you can do is pray daily for the salvation of Israel.

The other thing you can do is financially support ministries that are reaching out to the Jewish people. Jewish Voice, the ministry I lead, is only one of many that do a wonderful job of proclaiming the Gospel to the Jewish people. Ask God to reveal which ministries to support, but by all means, do support outreach to the Jewish people.

The great British Protestant missionary to China, Hudson Taylor (1832–1905), whom God used to transform China, always sent his first tithe of the year to a Jewish ministry in London. The Mildmay Missions to the Jews received a check from him each year with an inscription on the "memo line": *To the Jew first!*[1] He did this because he understood the relationship between the salvation of Israel and the salvation of China.

Ask the pastor or missions director of your church what percentage of its missions budget is used for reaching the Jewish people. If it is a tiny amount or none at all, then urge those in authority to consider re-ordering their priorities in light of the Gospel mandate that the Gospel is to the Jew first, and then to the Gentiles (Romans 1:16). Then take a look at your own giving and ask yourself what you could do to personally reach the lost sheep of Israel with the Good News.

Finally, pray for Israel. Someone told me a story not long ago that made me think of what happens when we pray for Israel. A man named Mark was in the hospital dying. Fever raged through his body. His blood pressure was dangerously low. Doctors tried everything they could to help him, but nothing worked. Experts were baffled by Mark's mysterious illness and finally walked away shaking their heads. Mark was a believer who prayed for healing, but his slide toward death continued.

Then he awakened in the middle of the night and noticed that he had a roommate. In the darkness of the room and the haze of his own fever, Mark could not discern much about the man who was across the room in the bed near the window, but what he could see made his heart drop. This poor fellow was in terrible shape. His arms looked as thin as pencils. His cheeks were sunken, his eyes hollow. An IV tube protruded from his arm.

Compassion flooded Mark's heart. "Lord," he prayed, "that man looks as if he is really suffering. Forget about me. If it is my time to die, I am ready. But please heal that guy." Mark fell asleep while he was still praying.

The next thing he knew a nurse was bringing his breakfast into his room. Sunshine streamed through the window. Mark had enjoyed his best sleep in days.

"You are looking so much better!" the nurse gasped.

"I feel better," he agreed.

When the nurse turned to leave the room, Mark saw that the bed next to the window was empty, and his heart sank.

"What happened to the other patient?" Mark called after her, "Did he die?"

She stopped suddenly, turned around and looked at him as if he had lost his mind. "What patient?"

"The man they put in the other bed last night. It broke my heart just to look at him."

Concern clouded her face. "There has not been anybody in this room but you," she said. "You must have been imagining things. I had better get the doctor. You know, with your fever . . ."

"I was not hallucinating," he insisted, pointing at the other bed. "He was right there in that . . ." Mark did not finish the sentence as the truth hit him.

There had not been anyone in that bed during the night. He now realized he had been looking at the window—and seeing his own reflection.

He had been praying for himself.

He had been filled with compassion for someone else and put the other patient's needs ahead of his own. God had responded, and he had been healed. Mark walked out of the hospital the next day changed in body and in spirit.

In the same way, when you pray for the salvation of God's chosen people—the physical descendants of Abraham, Isaac and Jacob—you are also praying for yourself, your family and your community. Their healing is your healing. Their salvation is your salvation. Their return to God is life from the dead for us all.

9

Rabbi, What More Can I Do?

People say to me, "You make it sound easy to reach Jews with the Gospel, but it is not."

Believe me; I know how resistant Jewish people can be.

My friend Sid Roth, host of the television program *It's Supernatural*, told me a story years ago that illustrates this point. It grieved Sid that his widowed father did not want to hear anything about Yeshua and, in fact, forbade his son to bring a New Testament into his home.

Sid thought long and hard about how to overcome his dad's resistance. Finally, inspiration hit. While attending his father's synagogue one day, he bought a kosher Jewish Publication Society version of the Hebrew Scriptures—a Jewish version of the Old Testament. He then asked the rabbi to sign it for him. That night he gave the Bible to his father as a gift. Then as they were sitting together, Sid said, "Dad, I want to read you something."

He turned to Isaiah 53 and read the entire chapter. When he finished, the old man's face reddened, and he said angrily, "I told you never to bring a New Testament into my home."

"But, Dad," Sid protested, "this is Isaiah 53 from our own Scriptures." He showed his father that he had been reading from a kosher Bible signed by his rabbi.

Sid's dad sat there for a moment or two, looking at that rabbi's signature. Finally he spoke: "I never trusted that rabbi."

Indeed, when it comes to considering the claims of Jesus as Messiah, Jewish attitudes can be deep-rooted. Their minds are already made up, so they do not want to be confused with the facts.

Furthermore, accepting Yeshua as the Messiah is an act that can leave a Jew cut off from his family, friends and culture. It is not a decision that can be made lightly.

I was raised in a Jewish home. All my parents' friends were Jewish. Although we lived in different areas of Rochester, the Jewish community was very ingrown. We had what I call an "us and them" mentality—we were Jews, and anyone who wasn't Jewish was a Gentile or Christian. They were synonymous. I was taught as a child that Christians did not like us and that they blamed us for killing their God, Jesus Christ. You can imagine my parents' shock and pain when I told them I had now accepted Him. I had become one of them. One of the first things they did was send me to the rabbi. And rather than deal with all the proofs I brought, he kept pushing the guilt button.

"Your grandfather would be rolling over in his grave if he knew you had done this," he said. "He would do anything to stop you."

In addition, he dispensed even more guilt with a follow-up letter connecting my faith to the Nazis' effort to destroy the Jewish people. "Just as Adolf Hitler tried to destroy us physically," he said, "you, by your rejection of Judaism and conversion to Christ, will destroy us spiritually."

I have heard Jewish people say, "You cannot be a Jew and believe in Jesus any more than you can be a vegetarian who

153

eats meat." It is not that they are belligerent. It is just that their worldview does not allow them to see how a Jew can believe in Jesus and remain a Jew, given two thousand years of persecution at the hands of those who called themselves Christians.

This is why it takes a special sensitivity and depth of understanding when talking to a Jewish person about Jesus.

How Do I Talk to a Jew about My Faith?

When believers ask me this question, as they often do, I respond with another question:

How do you share your faith with anyone?

First, you have to care enough to watch, listen and see what is going on in their lives. Our message has to be relevant, and we need to approach them where they are. If you can discover, for example, that the person with whom you are talking does not even believe in God, it is probably not going to be relevant to jump right in and convince them that Jesus is their Savior. If someone does not believe in sin, you do not want to begin by talking about how Jesus bore the sins of all mankind and proclaim to the person that he or she can be forgiven.

In the same way, you start witnessing to a Jewish person by listening to him or her. By demonstrating through your actions that you care. By letting your light shine so the person sees you have a special relationship with God. By offering to pray during his or her times of need.

The apostle Paul also gives us instruction on how to witness to the Jewish people. In Romans, Paul speaks of the Jewish community who had not embraced Yeshua as Messiah: "Have they stumbled that they should fall? God forbid: but rather through their fall salvation is come unto the Gentiles, for to provoke them to jealousy" (Romans 11:11, KJV).

What does it mean "to provoke [the Jewish people] to jealousy?" It means that we are to demonstrate the love, joy, peace and sense of purpose that comes through a relationship with God. This is the relationship they were destined to enjoy, and when they see these qualities in Christians and understand it is because of our personal relationship with the God of Israel—their God—they will be provoked to jealousy.

They may seem indifferent or even standoffish at the time, but watch what happens when trouble strikes. You will be the first one they call, asking, "Please pray for me." Many people who come to the Lord do so at such a point of crisis in their lives. They may have rejected the Gospel for years. They may have let you know in no uncertain terms that they do not want to hear another word about your faith. Then a tragedy strikes, and suddenly they begin to ask questions they were unwilling to face in the past.

To sum up what I am saying as simply as possible: *Never give up.* Those to whom you reach out (Jewish and Gentile alike) may be rude and reject you, but if you are always there, demonstrating unconditional love, then they will come to you in their time of need. Just be encouraged by the fact that the Word of God never returns to Him empty (Isaiah 55:11). It always accomplishes what God sent it to do.

Effective Communication

I believe with all my heart that the time to favor Zion is now! So expect to see results as you share your faith with your Jewish friends. But remember that only God can open a person's heart. Your job is to open your mouth and share effectively and sensitively.

To do that, I have prepared a short list of suggested language to use and not use to more effectively communicate when sharing Messiah with Jewish people. This is not to mask or conceal the truth of the message you are trying to share, but rather to communicate more accurately so Jewish people will better understand with greater clarity what you are trying to explain to them.

What you say is not what they hear

All too often, well-meaning believers communicate their faith using familiar language that is at best foreign to Jewish people and at worst offensive. Following are some of the most significant:

1. CONVERT OR CONVERSION

Although *conversion* is a biblical word meaning "to turn and go in the other direction," it means something quite different to Jewish people. To them it sounds like, "Stop being a Jew and become a Christian." We need to let Jewish people know that it is possible to be Jewish *and* believe in Yeshua. When you tell a Jew that he or she must "become a Christian," that person hears, "Leave the Jewish faith and embrace another religion." And that is *not* the message of the New Testament. That is *not* the Gospel, the Good News. We need to communicate that it is possible to remain a Jew and embrace Yeshua as Messiah.

God never intended for Christianity and Judaism to become separate religious institutions. I would love to hear Christians say to their Jewish friends, "I am not suggesting that you convert to another religion or change who you are. You were born a Jew and you will die a Jew. But Yeshua is your Messiah, and I want you to know Him."

At Jewish Voice, we are not trying to convert people from one culture or religion to another. Rather, we are trying to communicate to Jewish people in a language they understand that Yeshua is the promised Messiah of Israel, "the way, the truth and the life" (John 14:6), and that no one, Jew or Gentile, can come to the one true God except through Him. It is a message of *relationship*, not *religion*.

2. CHURCH

To the Jewish listener, the word *church* stands for another religious institution, and in many cases, a religion opposed to Jews and Judaism. *Church* is in direct contrast to *synagogue* and triggers that "us and them" mentality I spoke of earlier. It immediately conjures up thoughts of forced conversion and atrocities committed against the Jewish people in the name of Christ and Christianity. I greatly prefer *body of Messiah, followers of Yeshua* or *followers of Jesus*.

The word *church* is translated from the Greek word *ekklesia*, which comes from two words *ek* meaning "out" and *kaleo* meaning "to call." In fact, the Church is not a religious institution, but biblically represents those who have been called out by the Spirit of God, and according to the declaration of Jesus in Matthew 16, speaks of those who, like Peter, have received the revelation that Yeshua is the Messiah, the *Christos*, which means "the Anointed One."

> [Jesus] said to them, "But who do you say that I am?" Simon Peter answered and said, "You are the Christ, the Son of the living God." Jesus answered and said to him, "Blessed are you, Simon Bar-Jonah, for flesh and blood has not revealed this to you, but My Father who is in heaven. And I also say to you that you are Peter, and on this rock I will build My Church [Ekklesia], and the gates of Hades [hell] shall not prevail against it."
>
> Matthew 16:15–18, NKJV

The ekklesia are those individuals throughout the ages who have entered into this relationship through the revelation of God's Spirit and are now born from above. This is the essence of what must be communicated with Jew and non-Jew alike when we share our faith. Again, it is about relationship—not religion. I cannot stress this point enough. The word *church* should be carefully explained in this fashion to a Jewish person.

3. BAPTIZE OR BAPTISM

Another word that means something different to the Jewish listener is the word *baptize*. To a Jewish person, the word *baptize* immediately says "convert to Christianity and leave behind Judaism." This word association is the result of a two-thousand-year history of efforts to force Jews to convert to Christianity by the edge of the sword. Baptism, then, denotes forced conversion to Christianity, and by being baptized, a Jewish person believes he or she is actually leaving behind Judaism and is becoming something else.

The word *baptize* comes from the Greek word *baptiso*, "to immerse." When John *immersed* people in preparation for the coming of the Messiah, his understanding and the understanding of those who followed him were quite different from today. You see, immersion is, in fact, part of ancient Judaism. The Hebrew word for immersion is *tefillah* and is directly connected to a *mikvah*, or "ritual bath." In Judaism, mikvah is a bath used for the purpose of ritual immersion or cleansing. Women, for example, would go through the mikvah after their period of uncleanness—their menstrual cycle. Couples would be immersed in the mikvah prior to marriage. Jews would immerse themselves in the mikvah prior to entering the Temple.

It is important to explain the Jewish origins of immersion and that when one does go through the waters of immersion as described in the New Testament, they are not converting to another religion. Rather, they are identifying with the death, burial and resurrection of the Messiah.

It is preferable, therefore, to avoid the word *baptize* altogether and instead use *tefillah* or *immersion* and explain how this was part of Jewish practice long before the New Testament.

4. CHRIST

When I heard the term *Christ* as a boy, it was used 1) as a swear word, or 2) in reference to the God of Christianity, Jesus Christ, the son of Mr. and Mrs. Christ. In other words, I understood that Jesus was His first name and Christ was His last name, or family name.

My understanding was not unusual. To most Jewish people, Christ has nothing whatsoever to do with Judaism. This name represents the God of a completely different religion—the religion of Christianity.

The word *Christ* comes from another Greek word, *Christos*, which simply means "the Anointed One." The Hebrew word for "Anointed One" is *Maschiach*, or *Messiah*.

Now I understand, of course, that *Christos* is His title. He is *Yeshua* ("God's salvation") and *Christos* ("The Anointed One" or *Messiah*). The correct way to say this in Hebrew would be Yeshua HaMashiach. When speaking with a Jewish person, the use of the word *Messiah* instead of *Christ* immediately makes this a Jewish issue for the listener. Even when using Jesus rather than Yeshua, which I do frequently, I never say Christ when I am sharing with Jewish people. I refer to Him as Jesus, the Messiah.

5. THE SYMBOL OF THE CROSS

The cross is a negative symbol to Jewish people. For Jews, the cross does not represent sacrifice and atonement, as it does for Christians. Rather, the cross represents a two-thousand-year legacy of hatred and atrocities committed by those who called themselves Christians.

As the Crusaders marched across Europe during the Middle Ages, they massacred Jewish communities all along the way, and at the front of their armies, they carried a banner that featured the cross. The cross also reminds Jews of the Spanish Inquisition, when they were forced by the edge of the sword to convert to Christianity or be killed. Then there is the Holocaust. Nazi soldiers' uniforms, which bore crosses, albeit crooked ones, implied that "we kill you because you killed Jesus Christ." In fact, some Jews were marched into gas chambers under signs that read, "You are being killed in the name of Jesus Christ." Horrible, but true.[1]

The Messianic Jewish version of the Bible, which was translated by my good friend David Stern, replaces *cross* with *execution stake* or *tree*, which is consistent with prophecy and in many cases with the Greek references. Messianic Jews will often say "tree."

I am not afraid to talk about the cross and want to respect Christians who place great value on the symbol of the cross. I certainly understand the significance of the atonement and what the cross represents biblically. But I want to make clear what the word means to the Jewish people and help Christians understand the effect the mention and symbol of the cross have on Jewish people. A focus on the cross actually undercuts the message for the Jewish listener because of what it represents to them.

What should I say that they will hear?

In addition to the things to avoid when sharing with Jewish people, I also want to share some do's as well.

1. HELP YOUR JEWISH FRIENDS TO LEARN WHO YESHUA REALLY IS AND TO UNDERSTAND THAT HE DID NOT COMMIT THE ATROCITIES COMMITTED AGAINST THE JEWISH PEOPLE.

In chapter 2, I discussed the persecution the Jewish people have undergone in the name of "Christ" and "Christianity." As a result of such atrocities, Jewish people will often respond, "How can you ask me to believe in a person who is responsible for so much Jewish bloodshed? I would be a traitor to my fathers who died if I renounced their religion and accepted Jesus."

We must help our Jewish friends and neighbors understand who Jesus really was and is. He is Yeshua, the promised Jewish Messiah. Then we must help them understand that the people who carried out these horrible acts were not true Christians. In fact, they were going against everything Jesus taught and lived by.

We must help them see that not only is Jesus an option for them, but the Gospel is first for them. His earthly ministry was devoted to His Jewish brethren. We must show them that Yeshua was and is the One promised in the Torah and foretold by the Jewish prophets in the Jewish Scriptures.

2. Share the Gospel from the Hebrew Scriptures.

For the Jewish people, there is no New Testament. Their only Scriptures are what Christians call the Old Testament. When I refer to the Hebrew Scriptures, therefore, I am talking about the Old Testament.

The Hebrew name for the Old Testament is Tanakh. This name is derived from the initials of the three sections of the Hebrew Scriptures: the Law (Torah—*T*), the Prophets (Nevi'im—*N*) and the Writings (Ketuvim—*K*). Thus, *T*, *N* and *K* combine to make the word *Tanakh*.

It has been said—and rightly so—that the New Testament is *concealed* in the Old Testament and the Old Testament is *revealed* in the New. In Luke 24:27 Yeshua pointed to the Hebrew Scriptures to prove He was the Messiah. Acts 28:23 says the apostles expounded on the Scriptures to show that Jesus was the promised Messiah. To what Scriptures were they referring? The Hebrew Scriptures, or the Tanakh, of course. Remember that there was no New Testament at that time; it did not yet exist. They were using the Tanakh to prove that Yeshua was, in fact, the Jewish Messiah, the One proclaimed throughout the Torah, the Prophets, and the Writings of the Hebrew Scriptures.

The Tanakh, or Old Testament, is the story of man's sin and resulting separation from God. From the first chapters of Genesis through the last sentence of Malachi, the Old Testament shows mankind's need for a Redeemer and sets the stage for His arrival. More than three hundred Messianic prophecies are contained in the Tanakh. Foundational biblical doctrines such as the virgin birth, atonement for sin, righteousness through faith, covering of sin through blood sacrifice, heaven and hell, the rejection of Messiah by His own people and then their ultimate acceptance of Him—all are found in the pages of the Hebrew Scriptures. They are specific details written hundreds of years before Yeshua was ever born. Yeshua fulfilled many of these in connection with His First Coming. The remaining prophecies will be fulfilled upon His return. It is vital to use Old Testament prophecies and not just the New Testament when sharing the Gospel with Jewish people.

A common misconception among Christians is that Jewish people will know their own Scriptures. This is absolutely untrue. The fact is that most Jewish people have never read the Scriptures upon which they claim to base their religion and faith. According to recent statistics, only about 10 percent of Jews in America and a maximum of 20 percent of Jews worldwide have any sort of knowledge of their own Scriptures.

They reject Yeshua not because they have studied the facts but because they have been told to reject Him by their parents and rabbi. They do not know why. They just do as they are told. With your help, this can change.

3. Share key Messianic prophecies.

As I said, the Scriptures contain hundreds of Messianic prophecies, but I use a handful over and over again that I have found most helpful in witnessing to my Jewish brethren. One of my favorites is a riddle:

> Who has gone up to heaven and come down?
> Who has gathered up the wind in the hollow of his hands?
> Who has wrapped up the waters in his cloak?
> Who has established all the ends of the earth?
> What is his name, and the name of his Son?
> Tell me if you know!
>
> Proverbs 30:4

This is an amazing passage that Jewish people will really find challenging if they read it objectively. It is obviously referring to God and clearly states that He has a unique Son.

Next, Isaiah 53 is an amazingly accurate and vivid picture of the Messiah being rejected and suffering:

> Surely He has borne our griefs and carried our sorrows; yet we esteemed Him stricken, smitten by God, and afflicted. But He was wounded for our transgressions, He was bruised for our iniquities; the chastisement for our peace was upon Him, and by His stripes we are healed. All we like sheep have gone astray; we have turned, every one, to his own way; and the Lord has laid on Him the iniquity of us all. He was oppressed and He was afflicted, yet He opened not His mouth; He was led as a lamb to the slaughter, and as a sheep before its shearers is silent, so He opened not His mouth. He was taken from prison and from judgment, and who will declare His generation? For He was cut off from the land of the living; for the transgressions of My people He was stricken. And they made His grave with the wicked—but with the rich at His death, because He had done no violence, nor was any deceit in His mouth.
>
> Isaiah 53:4–9, NKJV

This is the Scripture that my friend Sid Roth read to his father, and it had an obvious effect on him. This passage from the Hebrew Scriptures was written more than 750 years before Yeshua was born.

Another Scripture I love to use is Psalm 22, a powerful portrayal of Yeshua's crucifixion. If read with an open mind, it is impossible not to be moved by this Scripture's depiction of the suffering He endured as He died for the sins of mankind:

My God, My God, why have You forsaken Me? Why are You so far from helping Me, and from the words of My groaning? O My God, I cry in the daytime, but You do not hear; and in the night season, and am not silent. But You are holy, enthroned in the praises of Israel. Our fathers trusted in You; they trusted, and You delivered them. They cried to You, and were delivered; they trusted in You, and were not ashamed. But I am a worm, and no man; a reproach of men, and despised by the people. All those who see Me ridicule Me. . . . But You are He who took Me out of the womb; You made Me trust while on My mother's breasts. I was cast upon You from birth. From My mother's womb You have been My God.

Be not far from Me, for trouble is near; for there is none to help. Many bulls have surrounded Me . . . like a raging and roaring lion. I am poured out like water, and all My bones are out of joint. . . . You have brought Me to the dust of death. . . . They pierced My hands and My feet; I can count all My bones. They look and stare at Me. They divide My garments among them, and for My clothing they cast lots.

Psalm 22:1–18, NKJV

Yet another passage I use depicts the specific place and time of Yeshua's birth. Bethlehem was just a little village—of no consequence—except that it was the birthplace of King David. But unimportant as it was, it is clearly mentioned as the birthplace of the Messiah. Some would argue that this passage is speaking

of King David, but it is a predictive prophecy that was written after David was long gone. Not only that, but it also tells us that although He would be born, His existence would be from old—from everlasting. It therefore speaks to the preexistence of the Messiah.

> "But you, Bethlehem Ephrathah, though you are small among the clans of Judah, out of you will come for me one who will be ruler over Israel, whose origins are from of old, from ancient times." Therefore Israel will be abandoned until the time when she who is in labor gives birth. . . . He will stand and shepherd his flock in the strength of the Lord. . . . His greatness will reach to the ends of the earth. And he will be their peace.
>
> Micah 5:2–5

Daniel 9:24–27 is another powerful one. Here we are told that the Messiah would have to come before the destruction of the second Temple:

> Seventy weeks are determined for your people and for your holy city, to finish the transgression, to make an end of sins, to make reconciliation for iniquity, to bring in everlasting righteousness, to seal up vision and prophecy, and to anoint the Most Holy. . . . [F]rom the going forth of the command to restore and build Jerusalem until Messiah the Prince, there shall be seven weeks and sixty-two weeks; the street shall be built again, and the wall, even in troublesome times. And after sixty-two weeks Messiah shall be cut off, but not for Himself . . . and the people of the prince who is to come shall destroy the city and the sanctuary. . . . Then he shall confirm a covenant with many for one week; but in the middle of the week He shall bring an end to sacrifice and offering. And on the wing of abominations shall be one who makes desolate, even until the consummation, which is determined, is poured out on the desolate.
>
> Daniel 9:24–27, NKJV

Not only does this prophecy tell us Messiah would die before the Temple was destroyed (which means that He had to come before AD 70, when the Temple was destroyed by the Romans), but it also tells us that He would be "cut off—but not for Himself." This is amazing! Literally, in the Hebrew, it says He would die for the transgressions of others, rather than for His own. I see this directly connecting to Isaiah 53, which says that He was bruised for our iniquities and the chastisement of our peace was upon Him. He was cut off (in other words, He was killed), but not for Himself.

Other excellent Scriptures to use are Isaiah 7:14, Jeremiah 31:31–34 and Zechariah 12:10. Again, there are hundreds of other amazing prophecies—many already fulfilled in connection with Yeshua's First Coming—but the ones I have presented here are the ones I use most often and suggest that you know as well, in order to be more a effective witness to your Jewish friends.

4. ADDRESS THE TRINITY AND YESHUA'S DIVINITY.

One of the biggest objections Jewish people have with regard to Yeshua is His claim of divinity. They claim that no passages in the Hebrew Scriptures indicate the Messiah will be anything more than a man. He will be a special man, they say. He will be anointed. But He will not be divine. They also object to teachings on the Trinity and say that Christians believe in three gods, while Jews believe in only one.

I agree that *Trinity* is a less than ideal word in that it does seem to denote three. I much prefer to use the word Tri-Unity because it expresses a plurality, yet within a unity of one. The Hebrew Scriptures do hint many times that although God is one, He is expressed as a plurality within that Oneness. For example, in Genesis 1:26, the Hebrew actually says, "Let *Us* make man in *Our* own image, in *Our* likeness." One could argue that this is the plurality of majesty, but a good case can also be made for the plurality within unity.

Micah 5, which we have already discussed, again mentions that this Ruler, although He would be born in Bethlehem, would be from old, from everlasting. The idea of the preexistence of the Messiah was a concept vaguely understood, yet embraced by the ancient rabbis.

Another indicator of this plurality within unity is the very word used for "one." It is the Hebrew word *echad*, as opposed to the Hebrew word *yachid*. When *yachid* is mentioned, it is as an absolute indivisible one, but *echad* is used in various places to express this plurality within unity. Numbers 13:23, for example, tells us, "When they reached the Valley of Eshcol, they cut off a branch bearing a single cluster of grapes. Two of them carried [that single cluster] on a pole between them, along with some pomegranates and figs." The word translated "single" here is *echad*—one single cluster composed of many grapes.

When we are told in Genesis 2:24 that a man shall leave his mother and father and cling to his wife, and the two shall become one flesh, the Hebrew word for one flesh is *besar echad*, or two becoming one—two entities—yet spiritually existing as one.

A third hint is the very word translated God, *Elohim*, which is plural. *Eloah*, a singular name for God, is used in Scripture, but *Elohim* is used far more—even ten times more. Even in the very first verses of the Torah, God is expressed in the plural and is delineated as the Father and the Spirit. Genesis 1:1–3, for example, says:

> In the beginning Elohim created the heavens and the earth. Now the earth was formless and empty, darkness was over the surface of the deep, and the Spirit of Elohim was hovering over the waters. And Elohim said, "Let there be light," and there was light.

A final interesting Scripture worth noting is Isaiah 48:16: "Come near to me, hear this: I have not spoken in secret from the beginning; from the time that it was, I was there. And now the LORD God and his Spirit have sent me." This is a fascinating verse that contains this Tri-Unity: Father, Son and Spirit.

For further biblical proof that Jesus is the Messiah, I encourage you to read another of my books, *A Rabbi Looks at Jesus of Nazareth*.

5. SHOW THAT YOU REALLY CARE.

Someone once told me that people do not care what you know until they know you care. I have never forgotten this. In fact, it has been a guiding principle in my life and ministry.

In the book of James, we are asked this important question:

> Suppose a brother or sister is without clothes and daily food. If one of you says to him, "Go, I wish you well; keep warm and well fed," but does nothing about his physical needs, what good is it?
>
> James 2:15–16

John asks the same question:

> If anyone has material possessions and sees his brother in need but has no pity on him, how can the love of God be in him? Dear children, let us not love with words or tongue but with actions and in truth.
>
> 1 John 3:17–18

At Jewish Voice, one of the primary ways we reach out to Jewish people is to provide medical clinics in countries such as Ethiopia, Zimbabwe and India. We offer essential medical care, dental care, eye care, eye glasses, eye surgery and medicines. Last year we provided medical care to more than thirty thousand people in need—all completely free of charge. At the conclusion of our medical services, we offer them an opportunity to visit our prayer room to hear more about why we have come. A large percentage of these people respond positively, and thousands of people pray with us to receive the Lord.

Jewish people are like anyone else. They respond to people who they feel care about them as a person and demonstrate that care and concern consistently, over time.

6. BELIEVE FOR MIRACLES.

As we reach out with God's love, we often find that He confirms His Word with miracles. I could give you many examples, but let me share one that happened a couple of years ago in Gondar, Ethiopia. We have been working in Gondar for many years, helping people living in total squalor.

To give you a little background, these are Ethiopian people of Jewish ancestry who are hoping one day to make aliyah, to immigrate to Israel. But they are extremely poor, and it will be a struggle for Israel to assimilate them. (One of every three Israelis lives in poverty, and the country is understandably reluctant to bring in more families who will need assistance.) Some of these Ethiopian Jews have been living in camps for twenty years or more. They have almost nothing except the clothes they wear. Although the elders of the community are happy to have us provide help for their people, they are also wary because they fear that associating with anyone who is seen as a potential threat to them, such as Christians and Messianic Jews, might cause the Israeli government to refuse them for immigration to Israel.

One of those who came to us for help was a young man in his late teens who had been deaf and mute his entire life. He had never uttered a single word, nor had he ever heard one.

Medically, our doctors confirmed that there was nothing we could do to help him, but we could—and did—pray for him. And when we did, God performed a miracle.

It is impossible to describe the amazed look on the young man's face when he began to hear other people's voices. Imagine being nearly twenty years old and never having heard a sound in your life, then hearing sound for the first time. His eyes bugged out as if he were terrified, but after a few moments, when he realized what was going on, his face lit up with a huge grin.

I felt like I was living out the book of Acts. The elders of that community had known that young man his entire life. There was no denying that he had been deaf, and now he could hear.

In front of the elders, I stood behind the young man and whispered "Yeshua" into his ear. Without any hesitation, he repeated it audibly. I then said in his other ear, "Shalom." He immediately repeated, again without hesitation, "Shalom." I could see the look of consternation on the faces of the elders who had known him for his entire life. They knew something was different. As a result of that miracle, a number of these elders have since become believers in Yeshua.

The miracles of God are definitely effective tools for bringing Jewish people into relationship with Him. In fact, we are told in 1 Corinthians 1:22 that the Jews require a sign. Nothing has changed since the time that this was written.

7. Pray for your Jewish friends.

I am convinced that God does nothing apart from the prayers of His people. Prayer, over time, can change a person's heart. Time and time again, I have witnessed Jewish people who were openly hostile toward me and my message at first completely change their attitude as a direct result of prayer. I am often asked by Christians for advice on how they can share their faith with their Jewish friends, many of whom are not really open to hear about Jesus. My immediate reply is always to pray for them by name every day. Many have reported back that as they faithfully prayed for them, they witnessed a growing openness, and some have even been able to eventually lead their Jewish friends to the Lord!

Paul, speaking to the church at Rome, declared in Romans 10:1, "Brethren, my heart's desire and *prayer to God* for the Israelites is that they may be saved" (emphasis added). As the apostle to the Gentiles, what would his purpose be for sharing this with them, risking that some might be offended that *they* were not the focus of his prayer and center of his concern? I believe it was to motivate those who loved him and looked to him for leadership to share this burden with him and to join him in praying for the salvation of his brothers in the natural.

In Isaiah 62:6–7 we are exhorted to give the Lord no rest until He fulfills His plan to again make Jerusalem a praise in all the earth:

I have set watchmen on your walls, O Jerusalem; they shall never hold their peace day or night. You who make mention of the LORD, do not keep silent, and give Him no rest till He establishes and till He makes Jerusalem a praise in the earth.

NKJV

This is a plea for those who know Him, who call upon His name, to faithfully intercede for the land and people of Israel. As those who know the truth, we are entrusted to be as watchmen, spiritual protectors and guardians of the Jewish people through prayer.

We see a similar exhortation in the Psalms, where we are instructed to "Pray for the peace of Jersualem" In fact, we are also told that as a direct result of one's faithfulness to do this, prosperity will follow: "Pray for the peace of Jerusalem: they shall prosper that love thee" (Psalm 122:6, KJV). The word translated *peace* in this verse is the Hebrew word *shalom* and can also mean "well-being" or "completion." I believe this verse is encouraging us to pray that God's true plan for this land and people be brought to completion. We know that this peace plan is the revelation of His Son, the Prince of Peace to Jew and Arab, Israeli and Palestinian alike. Only then can there be true peace. And the only way this can be brought about is through prayer. Every one of us has a call and a responsibility before God to pray regularly for Israel and for the Jewish people God has brought into your life. They are *not* there by accident.

Expect Success

The Bible is not about religion. It is about relationship. And every time you share your faith or demonstrate God's love to a Jewish person, you are planting a seed that will not return void.

The most important thing to keep in mind is that this is a spiritual battle, and the truths of God are spiritually discerned. Romans 11:25 describes this clearly in relation to the Jewish people:

> I do not desire, brethren, that you should be ignorant of this mystery, lest you should be wise in your own opinion, that blindness in part has happened to Israel *until* the fullness of the Gentiles has come in.

> Romans 11:25, NKJV (emphasis added)

For almost two thousand years, a spirit of blindness has covered the eyes of the Jewish people. As we have discussed, one of the great signs of the last days is the blindness coming off their eyes. The fact that more Jewish people believe in Yeshua today than at any time since the first century is ironclad proof that we are living in these last days. The little word *until* clearly indicates that God has ordained a time for their blindness to be removed, and that time is now. In light of this, expect that God will use you and that you will see results over time when you share your faith with the Jewish people God has put into your life.

In closing this chapter, I want to relate the words of a friend who has gone home to be with the Lord. His name is Moishe Rosen, the founder of Jews For Jesus. He once told me, "Your only job is to open your mouth and share your faith. Only God can open their hearts."

Our job is to share our faith in word and deed. I promise you that as you do this and pray for them, God will do the rest.

10

A Step Further

I will make you into a great nation
and I will bless you;
I will make your name great,
and you will be a blessing.
I will bless those who bless you,
and whoever curses you I will curse;
and all peoples on earth
will be blessed through you.

Genesis 12:2–3

In the latter days of the fifteenth century, Spain was the world's preeminent power. Christopher Columbus sailed to the New World under the Spanish flag, and Spain quickly gained a foothold there.

But it was also during this time that Spain turned against the Jews. As we discussed in chapter 2, thousands of Jews were forcibly expelled from the country, and many more were tortured and killed during the Spanish Inquisition.

And almost immediately, Spain's fortunes began to decline. With the utter destruction of the Spanish Armada less than 100 years later, Spain's fall from power was complete.

Was this an example of Genesis 12 at work? I believe it was.

Consider what happened to Germany during and after World War II. Hitler brought on a war that killed 7.5 million German citizens (11 percent of Germany's population) and left behind a devastated, divided country whose agricultural production was reduced to only 35 percent of what it was before the war. The Allies ceded roughly 25 percent of Germany's pre-Anschluss territory to Poland and the Soviet Union. Much of the German population was scattered throughout Eastern Europe. Millions of German prisoners of war were used for several years as forced labor by both the Western Allies and the Soviets. Immediately after the German surrender and continuing for two years, the U.S. harvested all German technological and scientific knowledge, as well as German patents. And under the Marshall Plan, Germany's economic recovery was extremely slow.[1]

In recent years, however, Germany has experienced a reunification and financial prosperity in large part due to the repentance made by German Christians and their commitment to offering restitution to Holocaust survivors and the State of Israel on behalf of the Jewish people.

Then you have the example of Great Britain. It used to be said that the sun never set on the British Empire. During the nineteenth century, England dominated the world. Then, in 1917, they gained control of much of the Middle East when they defeated the Turks, including what was then Palestine. After reneging on a promise to help establish a Jewish homeland in Palestine, they began to limit Jewish emigration, and during and after World War II actually arrested concentration camp survivors trying to make their way to the Promised Land and Jews seeking to escape the Nazis. Today, the British Empire is only a shadow of what it once was. I am convinced this is a consequence of how they treated the Jews and Israel.

Radio personality Dennis Prager writes,

> Look at who most blesses the Jews and who most curses them, and you decide whether [or not] the verse in Genesis has validity. . . . It is the Arab world that curses the Jews. It rivals Nazi Germany for the ubiquity and intensity of its Jew-hatred. Look at its state. According to Arab scholars, appointed by the United Nations to report on the state of Arab society, that part of the world lags behind the rest of humanity, including in most instances sub-Saharan Africa, in virtually every social, moral and intellectual indicator. And there is no question but that its half-century-long preoccupation with destroying Israel has only increased the Arab world's woes.[2]

The decree of Genesis 12:2–3 continues to be in force, and modern history bears this out. If a country blesses Israel, then that country will be blessed. But if a country curses (harms or does not support) Israel, then God will lift His hand of protection, and that country will be cursed; that is, the country will no longer come under the providential protection and hand of God.

United States: Blessed or Cursed?

My friend Bill Koenig wrote a book a few years ago called *Eye to Eye*,[3] in which he presented compelling evidence that whenever the United States has sought to force Israel to give up land for peace or intervene in Israel's sovereignty as a nation, corresponding judgments such as floods, hurricanes, terrorist attacks and economic downturns have affected the U.S. The premise of the book, based upon Genesis 12:2–3, is that God's blessing or cursing of our nation has been clearly tied to our treatment of Israel and the Jewish people.

Koenig offers historical fact after fact indicating that every time the U.S. pressures Israel to give up land in exchange for peace, something terrible happens to our country. God is making His position clear: He is against man's efforts to bring about a false peace, and we are to take His eternal covenant with Israel seriously.

Even in the last few years, numerous instances have occurred where the U.S. did not support Israel and God's sovereignty was displayed. Here is just one example of what Bill's research uncovered:

May–August 2011: President Obama creates a firestorm when he calls for a new state to be based on "1967 borders with agreed upon land swaps." This unprecedented demand is announced just as Israel's Prime Minister Benjamin Netanyahu is en route to the United States for talks with Obama. It creates a rather tense situation. Upon arriving in the U.S., Netanyahu makes it clear in a news conference from the White House that these conditions are unacceptable to Israel, as it would be left with indefensible borders that would threaten its security and very survival.[4] Shortly thereafter, an EF4 "monster tornado" with winds ranging between 166 and 200 mph and a nearly one-mile wide funnel touches down in Joplin, Missouri, killing 116 people and injuring 500 others. It is the deadliest single tornado in nearly sixty years, according to federal records. Nearly 30 percent of the city of Joplin is damaged by the twister, with highly populated areas hit by the storm.[5]

A few months later, August 20–29, Hurricane Irene makes landfall over coastal North Carolina and moves northward, causing torrential rainfall, flooding, wind damage and lost power across the Northeast. Numerous tornadoes were reported in several states, further adding to the damage. The U.S. suffered at least 45 deaths and more than seven billion dollars in damages.

These major natural disasters greatly affected our nation, and the timing is not a coincidence. As the U.S. ordered Israel to make peace in the Middle East by giving up its land, and as an international attempt to delegitimize Israel escalated, the National Climatic Data Center (NCDC) reported that the U.S. sustained economic damage costs exceeding $45 billion in 2011.

Am I saying that God killed all those innocent people in order to teach the U.S. a lesson? Not at all. I do not think for a moment that God sent these calamities upon the American people. Instead, I believe He lifted His hand of protection, and we were battered by one disaster after another. Only God knows what would befall our nation if He completely lifted His protection from us. Only in the world to come will we know how often He has stretched out His hand to protect us, individually and as a nation.

Furthermore, during Obama's first three years in office, his administration, led by the president and Secretary of State Hillary Clinton, put a great deal of pressure on Israel to settle for peace in a way that potentially brought peril to Israel. Also during those three years, the country experienced more FEMA disasters, including twelve major insurance disasters costing more than one billion dollars each, than any other full-term (four-year) presidential administration.[6]

Example after example are cited in *Eye to Eye*. It is clear when you read this that God is not silent. He is speaking up loudly on this issue for those who have ears to hear. I recommend you read Bill's book to see how clearly God is weighing in on this issue.

One thing is certain: God's continued blessing and protection over us as a nation is directly connected to our blessing and support of the Jewish people and the nation of Israel.

We Are Called to Bless the Jews

God's biblical decree to bless the Jewish people is clear. Those who do so will be blessed, and those who do not will be cursed.

This mandate is just as real today as it was when it was written more than four thousand years ago. History has borne it out, and the principle continues to manifest to this day.

Why should we bless the Jewish people? The apostle Paul is clear about this when he declares:

> For I could wish that I myself were cursed and cut off from Christ for the sake of my brothers, those of my own race, the people of Israel. Theirs is the adoption as sons; theirs the divine glory, the covenants, the receiving of the law, the Temple worship and the promises. Theirs are the patriarchs, and from them is traced the human ancestry of [Messiah], who is God over all, forever praised! Amen.
>
> Romans 9:3–5

This raises an important question that I am often asked: Do you believe, then, that as a Christian I am unequivocally obligated to support every action taken by the State of Israel?

Absolutely not. The reality is that the vast majority of Israel's citizens are secular and have little belief in God. The government of Israel does not act as God's infallible agent. The Israeli government can and does make decisions that should be criticized. Nevertheless, the restoration of the Jewish people to the land is a divine fulfillment of biblical prophecy, and we must support this divine venture.

Despite the fact that most Israelis are living outside of a relationship with their God and, of course, His Messiah, God has kept His word to Abraham that this land was to be an eternal possession. Israel's right to the land is a divine land grant that we, as believers in the Bible, must support.

This does not mean that God loves the Jew more than the Arab—the Israeli more than the Palestinian. It is not about preference or loving one and hating the other. God loves everyone equally and desires that none should perish, but that all should find everlasting life (see John 3:16). He is not a respecter of persons. This is about God's faithfulness to an everlasting decree that He made with Abraham and his descendants. And God remains faithful to that promise and to His Word.

This promise is mentioned numerous times throughout Scripture, so there can be no doubt as to its interpretation. To Abraham, God said:

> And the LORD appeared unto Abram, and said, Unto thy seed will I give this land: and there builded he an altar unto the Lord, who appeared unto him.
>
> Genesis 12:7, KJV

> For all the land which thou seest, to thee will I give it, and to thy seed for ever. And I will make thy seed as the dust of the earth: so that if a man can number the dust of the earth, then shall thy seed also be numbered.
>
> Genesis 13:15–16, KJV

> And when Abram was ninety years old and nine, the LORD appeared to Abram, and said unto him, I am the Almighty God; walk before me. . . . And I will make my covenant between me and thee, and will multiply thee exceedingly. . . . [T]hou shalt be a father of many nations. Neither shall thy name any more be called Abram, but thy name shall be Abraham; for a father of many nations have I made thee. And I will make thee exceeding fruitful, and I will make nations of thee, and kings shall come out of thee. And I will establish my covenant between me and thee and thy seed after thee in their generations for an everlasting covenant, to be a God unto thee, and to thy seed after thee. And I will give unto thee, and to thy seed after thee, the land wherein thou art a stranger, all the land of Canaan, for an everlasting possession; and I will be their God.
>
> Genesis 17:1–9, KJV

Your wife Sarah will bear you a son, and you will call him Isaac.
I will establish my covenant with him as an everlasting covenant
for his descendants after him.

Genesis 17:19

To Isaac, God said:

Stay in this land for a while, and I will be with you and will
bless you. For to you and your descendants I will give all these
lands and will confirm the oath I swore to your father Abraham.

Genesis 26:3

I will make your descendants as numerous as the stars in the sky
and will give them all these lands, and through your offspring
all nations on earth will be blessed.

Genesis 26:4

To Jacob, God said:

And God said to him, "I am God Almighty; be fruitful and
increase in number. A nation and a community of nations will
come from you, and kings will be among your descendants. The
land I gave to Abraham and Isaac I also give to you, and I will
give this land to your descendants after you."

Genesis 35:11–12, NKJV

Moses prayed to God and asked Him to keep His promise:

Remember your servants Abraham, Isaac and Israel, to whom
you swore by your own self: "I will make your descendants as
numerous as the stars in the sky and I will give your descendants
all this land I promised them, and it will be their inheritance
forever."

Exodus 32:13

Caleb claimed the promise made to him and his forefathers:

181

So on that day Moses swore to me, "The land on which your feet have walked will be your inheritance and that of your children forever, because you have followed the LORD my God wholeheartedly."

Joshua 14:9

Jehosophat stood up before the assembly at the Temple and said:

O our God, did you not drive out the inhabitants of this land before your people Israel and give it forever to the descendants of Abraham your friend?

2 Chronicles 20:7

The divine decree that all nations are to bless the Jewish people is equally clear in Scripture:

Now when Balaam saw that it pleased the LORD to bless Israel . . . the Spirit of God came upon him and he uttered his oracle:

"The oracle of Balaam son of Beor,
the oracle of one whose eye sees clearly,
the oracle of one who hears the words of God,
who sees a vision from the Almighty,
who falls prostrate, and whose eyes are opened:

"How beautiful are your tents, O Jacob,
your dwelling places, O Israel!

"Like valleys they spread out,
like gardens beside a river,
like aloes planted by the LORD,
like cedars beside the waters.
Water will flow from their buckets;
their seed will have abundant water.

"Their king will be greater than Agag;
their kingdom will be exalted.

"God brought them out of Egypt;
they have the strength of a wild ox.
They devour hostile nations
and break their bones in pieces;
with their arrows they pierce them.
Like a lion they crouch and lie down,
like a lioness—who dares to rouse them?

"May those who bless you be blessed
and those who curse you be cursed!"

Numbers 24:1–9

Pray for the peace of Jerusalem: "May those who love you be
secure. May there be peace within your walls and security within
your citadels. For the sake of my family and friends, I will say,
'Peace be within you.' For the sake of the house of the LORD
our God, I will seek your prosperity."

Psalm 122:6–9

For if the Gentiles have shared in the Jews' spiritual blessings, they owe it to the Jews to share with them their material
blessings.

Romans 15:27

It is clear that believers in Yeshua are to be a blessing to the
Jewish people. God commands it, and it is still true today.

How Do We Fulfill That Calling?

In a practical sense, how do we fulfill this calling in our own
lives? Everyone who reads this book can do a handful of tangible
things to be a conduit of blessing to the Jewish people.

1. Learn how to effectively share your faith with the Jewish people God has placed in your life and how to provoke them to jealousy.

The greatest thing that you can give a Jewish person is the blessing of eternal life. And the only means to obtain eternal life is to embrace the Good News of Messiah. We need to understand and embrace the truth that the Gospel is the power of God unto salvation to all who believe—to the Jew first and also to the Gentile (see Romans 1:16). The Gospel imperative cannot be interpreted any other way than literally that there is one name given under heaven by which we must be saved, and that is through the person of Yeshua. The people whom God has placed in your life are not there by accident. If you love the Jewish people and want to be a blessing to them, first and foremost, you need to share your faith.

It is a misconception that the Jewish people have rejected Jesus already. Rather, they simply have not heard a message they can understand. In another of my books, *A Rabbi Looks at Jesus of Nazareth*, I address many of the misconceptions Christians have about Jewish people, as well as misconceptions that Jewish people have about Christians. I wrote that book specifically to address these issues and help Christians to sensitively and effectively share their faith with their Jewish friends, neighbors and co-workers. I encourage you to read *A Rabbi Looks at Jesus of Nazareth* and other books that will help you to be the effective witness that God is calling you to be in the lives of those Jewish people around you.

Paul makes it clear in Romans 11 that God is not finished with the Jewish people. He teaches us that Israel's rejection of their Messiah is temporary, and that their temporary rejection has allowed the Gospel to go to the Gentiles. He says that the day will come in God's timetable when He will restore them. He tells us that their restoration will bring life from the dead.

He also tells us that we Christians are to provoke the Jews to jealousy.

What does that mean? Sadly, for almost two thousand years, the Church has not understood the meaning of this mandate. Rather than provoking the Jews to jealousy, they have simply provoked.

To provoke people to jealousy, you have to possess something they want but do not have. If your neighbor has a perfectly green lawn, for example, and your lawn is brown and patchy, you will likely wish you had your neighbor's lawn. The quality of their landscaping provokes you to jealousy. If you are a sports car enthusiast and someone pulls up to you in a Ferrari, you may be provoked to jealousy.

Provoking the Jews to jealousy begins by understanding what we have that they do not. This is, of course, a living relationship with God, the indwelling of the Holy Spirit, and the gift of eternal life through faith in Israel's Messiah.

The Jewish people were called as a chosen people and a royal priesthood. They were the inheritors of God's blessing and His divine call. They were given the responsibility by God Himself to be a light to the nations and to bring a revelation of Him—the one true God of the universe—to all mankind.

They experienced the *shekinah*—the glory of God—in a tangible way as they left Egypt and wandered in the wilderness. As they worshiped and made sacrifice in the Temple, and even in their captivity, they possessed the covenants. They were pre-destined to experience the presence and the provision of God. Now, in their ignorance and blindness, they have strayed, and many do not know God.

Most Jewish people, particularly those who live in the United States, have become secularized and have no knowledge of what is contained in their own Scriptures. They have strayed into liberalism, and the Judaism of today no longer even requires that they believe in God. Belief in God has been replaced with a commitment to perpetuate the survival of the Jewish people and to promote social justice. Even if they believe in God, they lack the personal relationship that we as followers of the Messiah experience.

It is, therefore, the love, peace, joy, sense of destiny and purpose reflected in our lives that will provoke not just the Jew but anyone who observes us to jealousy. The fruits of the Spirit that are manifested in our lives will always have greater impact than anything we say. It is the walk—not the talk—that will provoke those around us to want to know why we are so different.

We earn the right to share our faith by the demonstration of God's attributes through us. How we handle ourselves in the midst of a crisis, how we respond to those who belittle or offend us, our work ethic, and our consistent prayer for others will all have profound effects on those observing us. When Jewish friends ask why we are so peaceful in difficult situations, the door is opened for us to say, "Your God, the God of Israel—your Messiah, Yeshua, changed my life." We possess something our Jewish friends want.

The greatest gift any human can possess is the deposit of God's Spirit within us. When He who lives in us is manifested through us to others, then we will fulfill Paul's exhortation to provoke Jews to jealousy.

Let God's light shine through you at all times.

2. Pray for the salvation of the Jewish people.

When I accepted the Lord in 1980, it was through the consistent testimony of a friend and her invitation to that Bible study. Later, I found out that she had enlisted her Bible study and church to pray for me by name.

Since that day, I have believed that prayer is the key to transform lives. When I am asked by Christians how they can effectively minister to their Jewish friends, my response is always the same: "Pray for them!" Yes, pray for your Jewish friends by name because I am absolutely convinced that God answers prayer.

Paul's exhortation to the Church at Rome was to pray for the salvation of Israel. He himself declared, "Brothers, my heart's desire and prayer to God for Israel is that they may be saved" (Romans 10:1, NKJV). As a believer, you have something no one else has: a direct pipeline to the Lord. You have the ear of God, the Creator of all things. And He urges you to call upon Him in prayer.

How should you pray for them? The answer is to pray the way Paul instructed us to pray and how he prayed himself. His prayer for the Jewish people was specifically focused on their salvation. He begins with an astounding statement in Romans 9:1–3, when he declares, "I could wish that I myself were accursed from [Messiah] for my brethren, my countrymen, according to the flesh" (NKJV). He again reiterates this in Romans 10:1 when he writes, "Brethren, my heart's desire and prayer to God for Israel is that they may be saved."

Paul's heart cry to God was not that the Jewish people would return to the land, not that the Jewish people would escape persecution, but that the Jewish people would recognize their Messiah and come into the promise of eternal life. In fact, his entire focus on his teaching to the Church about God's plan for Israel is their ultimate acceptance of Yeshua. Romans 11 makes it clear that the blindness covering the eyes of the Jewish people is only for a season and the day will come when all Israel will be saved.

> For I do not desire, brethren, that you should be ignorant of this mystery, lest you should be wise in your own opinion, that blindness in part has happened to Israel until the fullness of the Gentiles has come in. And so all Israel will be saved, as it

is written: "The Deliverer will come out of Zion, and He will turn away ungodliness from Jacob; for this is My covenant with them, when I take away their sins."

Romans 11:25–27, NKJV

God is looking for Christians who will stand in the gap and pray for the salvation of the Jewish people, so that He can move on behalf of those prayers. It is my firm conviction that the prayers of God's people—the Church, or true Christians—will bring about the removal of this blindness from the Jewish people and usher in their ultimate acceptance of Yeshua.

3. Pray for the nation of Israel.

Not only should we be praying for the salvation of the Jewish people scattered around the world, but we are also exhorted in Scripture to pray specifically for the land of Israel, and even more specifically, for the city of Jerusalem, Israel's capital. On my television program, *Jewish Voice with Jonathan Bernis*, I end every program with the exhortation in Psalm 122:6 to "Pray for the peace of Jerusalem: they shall prosper that love thee" (KJV).

I am often asked in letters and emails, "How should we pray for Israel?" The answer is found in the Hebrew. The word translated "peace" is the Hebrew word *shalom*. Not only does it mean "peace," but more accurately, it means "wholeness and completion." When we are exhorted to pray for the shalom of Jerusalem (as representative of the entire nation), I believe that God wants us to pray for His fullness to come to the land and to the people of Israel. In other words, God wants to bring to completion His plan for Israel, destined before the foundation of the world, and when we pray for the peace of Jerusalem, we are praying for the revelation of the Prince of Peace. We are praying for God's ultimate fulfillment to come to that region.

We are setting ourselves in agreement with what God has already promised in His Word.

No peace plan of man will ever succeed. No initiative orchestrated by the United States, Europe or the U.N. will succeed. The only plan that will ever succeed is God's peace plan, and that peace is found in a relationship with the Prince of Peace, Jesus the Messiah. Only when a person finds this true peace in his or her heart can unity between Jew and Arab, Israeli and Palestinian, be accomplished.

I love these verses from the prophet Isaiah:

> For Zion's sake I will not keep silent, for Jerusalem's sake I will not remain quiet, till her righteousness shines out like the dawn, her salvation like a blazing torch. . . . I have posted watchmen on your walls, O Jerusalem; they will never be silent day or night. You who call on the LORD, give yourselves no rest, and give him no rest till he establishes Jerusalem and makes her the praise of the earth.
>
> Isaiah 62:1, 6–7

This is an amazing exhortation! All of us who know the Lord are watchmen, and we are instructed not to be silent, to take no rest and to give God no rest until He accomplishes His plan and His purpose for Israel and the Jewish people. It is talking about prayer, the weapon that God has placed into our hands. Prayer is powerful to the pulling down of strongholds. Prayer changes things. Prayer moves the hand of God. If you wish to fulfill your role as a lover of Israel and the Jewish people, you must make prayer a priority.

I urge you to make a daily commitment to pray for God's shalom. As you do, you can address some specific prayer points:

- Pray that Jewish people—the physical descendants of Abraham, Isaac and Jacob—around the world will come to know Yeshua as their Messiah and King.

- Pray that the Lord will open the eyes of those who hate Israel and the Jewish people and bring them into the truth.
- Pray against the spirit of anti-Semitism and hatred of Israel and the Jewish people.
- Pray for protection over the nation of Israel.
- Pray for the Israeli government, as well as American and world leaders, to stand with God's agenda for Israel.
- Pray for believers in the land who struggle daily with persecution and the reality of maintaining their faith and spreading the Good News to their brethren.

4. Make your voice heard in support of Israel.

Zechariah prophesied that the day would come when all nations of the earth would turn against Israel. The only nation that is a true friend to Israel today is the United States. Sadly, that support seems to be waning.

President Obama was the first president in U.S. history to publicly state (May 2011) that Israel should return to its pre-1967 borders. This would be an indefensible position for Israel. Changing demographics would make it impossible for them to comply with this demand. Are we seeing a shift in American policy toward Israel that will eventually lead to America's joining the ranks of those against Israel? Quite possibly.

If this happens (and I am deeply concerned that it will), Israel's last friend in the world will be the Church—true Christians who believe God and take Him at His Word. As American believers, we must assert ourselves and take advantage of our rights as citizens of this country. We must speak out loudly in support of Israel, not because we favor Jews over Arabs, but because the Bible is clear that this land was given as an everlasting possession to the children of Abraham, Isaac and

Jacob. As believers, we must assert our biblical worldview in this important debate.

There are those who would say that we are just fighting against Bible prophecy, so we should let it happen. I am not prepared to let this country go to hell in a handbasket, so to speak. As long as we are on this earth, we are called to occupy until He comes, and that means casting our votes and making our voices heard when it comes to areas that are important to God.

5. Support ministries that proclaim the Gospel to the Jewish people.

As we have discussed, many organizations, including Jewish Voice, have been raised up by God to proclaim the Gospel to the Jewish people. In particular, Messianic Jewish organizations are reaching out to their own people effectively. Before you make a donation to any of these organizations, however, I urge you to do some investigating to make certain that your money is going where you want it to go.

How much of what you give will go directly into ministry, and how much will be spent on overhead, fund-raising or other costs? Go online and check out the organization's mission statement. Who endorses them? Do they have approval from watchdog groups such as The Evangelical Council of Financial Accountability or Charity Navigator? Find out if their doctrinal statements support what you believe. Again, the greatest blessing you can give to a Jewish person is the blessing of the Gospel, so find out if the organization supports Jewish evangelism.

You may be surprised to learn how many organizations say they are connected to Israel but actually oppose bringing the Good News to Jewish people. In fact, some organizations raising money for Israel actually oppose the Gospel going to Jewish people. I am sure the last thing you want to do is invest your money in efforts to prevent Jews from hearing the Gospel.

I know of one example where a great deal of financial support went to help an ultra-orthodox orphanage in Israel. Although believers should always help hurting children—and especially orphans—I also know that ultra-orthodox Jews have a clear agenda to rid Israel of what they see as *the missionary threat*—and that includes expelling from the land all who believe in Yeshua as Messiah. They, therefore, would possibly be using these funds to this end. I would also be concerned that such support is being used to train these children to have negative attitudes about Jesus.

Another organization raises tens of millions of dollars every year to help impoverished Jews in Israel and the former Soviet Union. Virtually all that money comes from evangelical Christians. In fact, the leader of that particular group regularly speaks in Christian churches across the country. And yet, he writes, "The notion that Jews are damned without Christ and that only through him and Christianity can they find fulfillment is utterly rejected."[7] And "A Jew who accepts Jesus as Lord or Messiah effectively ceases to be a Jew. . . . He is like a defector who walked out on his God and his family."[8] And then there's this little tidbit: "From a Jewish point of view, Messianic Jews are a front for evangelical Christians who try to wean Jews away from their ancestral faith by lulling them into believing that they can accept Jesus as Lord and still remain Jewish."[9]

Would you want your dollars to go to an organization whose leader holds these beliefs? I certainly would not!

Make sure that your financial contributions go exactly where you want them to go—that they are used to bless the Jewish people both financially and spiritually. A first priority in your giving should be ministries that believe the same thing you do. We have a responsibility before the Lord to be good stewards and, therefore, cautious about where our money goes. So give generously, but be cautious.

6. Support charities that provide food, clothing and other services to Jewish communities who live in poverty.

Believe it or not, there are Jews around the world who live in horrible poverty. In the former Soviet Union, for example, some elderly Jews still live without heat and basic foods. At Jewish Voice, a primary focus is to bring much-needed medical, dental and eye care to impoverished Jewish communities, such as the Beta Israel and Beta Avraham in Ethiopia, the Bnei Menashe in Manipur and Mizoram, India. We are also finding other impoverished Jewish communities in places like Somaliland and Zimbabwe. In these nations, Jewish poverty is often perpetuated by anti-Semitism that blocks the doors to good employment, denies entrance to the best schools and basically keeps the Jewish people marginalized and in need. In Ethiopia, for example, the Jewish community has been forced into occupations that are considered taboo and disdained by the populations, such as pottery making, textile weaving and smithing.

Tragically, many Jews who make aliyah to Israel from these developing nations find the situation is not much better there. Because Israel is forced to invest more than 65 percent of its budget in defense, social programs tend to suffer, and that means a lack of essential medical, dental and eye care—and even food and housing for immigrants. Unemployment is high, and one-third of the Israeli people live below the poverty line.

I know it breaks God's heart to see His people living this way, and He wants us to do what we can to help them. He calls out to us in Isaiah 40:1: "Comfort, comfort my people."

But once again, when you consider your giving to bless the Jewish people, be sure to support organizations that are committed both to helping the Jewish people living in poverty and also to reaching Jewish people with the Gospel.

7. Support Jewish believers in the land of Israel.

I am heartened by the growth of what is referred to as the Christian Zionist movement—Christians who love the Jewish people and support their right to the land given to their forefathers by God Himself. As a Jewish believer, I am a great supporter of Israel and believe followers of the Lord should understand God's faithfulness to the Jewish people and His promise to restore them to their land in the last days. Christian Zionism is clearly a movement that God has raised up to fulfill a vital role assigned to the Church—the role of helping the Jewish people come back from the four corners of the earth to their covenant land. As much as I am an advocate of Christian Zionism, however, and as much as I, along with other Messianic Jewish leaders, appreciate their fine work, a real danger to which Christian Zionists are susceptible is falling into any form of Dual Covenant Theology.

Remember that Dual Covenant Theology puts forth the idea that Jews have a separate way to God. Liberal theologians, in an attempt to express solidarity with the Jewish people after the Holocaust, created the idea that the Abrahamic and Mosaic Covenants provided a separate path of salvation and that Jews therefore did not need the New Covenant. In other words, Dual Covenant Theology seeks to give Jewish people a free pass to heaven without following the biblical requirement to repent and believe in God's provision of salvation through Jesus the Messiah. Although the vast majority of Bible-believing Christians do not adhere to Dual Covenant Theology, it has seeped into the thinking of some Christians who love Israel and the Jewish people. Sadly, this thinking has moved some Christian Zionists away from Jewish evangelism.

As Bible believers, we must embrace Scripture in its entirety or not at all. If we believe the Bible, then we must accept that there is only one way to God, and that is through the Messiah,

Yeshua. He is the Way, the Truth and the Life, and *no one* comes to the Father except through Him (see John 14:6).

I am concerned that Christian Zionism, in a desire to love the Jewish people unconditionally, has failed to grasp this foundational truth. In many cases, Christian Zionist leaders have built strong relationships with Jewish leaders in both Israel and the U.S. at the cost of shunning their Messianic Jewish Brethren. This has resulted in a marginalizing of Messianic Jews in favor of high-profile Jewish leaders.

If you love the Jewish people and support Israel, you need to embrace your Jewish brethren first and foremost. We are your *mishpachah*, your "family." This is especially true of believers in Israel who must daily endure the attacks of the Orthodox establishment and, in some cases, lose their jobs, homes, businesses and credibility because of their faith.

First Corinthians 16:1–3 describes how the apostle Paul collected financial support from the Church abroad. It was clearly for the believers in Jerusalem.

> Now about the collection for God's people: Do what I told the Galatian churches to do. On the first day of the week, each one of you should set aside a sum of money in keeping with his income, saving it up, so that when I come no collections will have to be made. Then, when I arrive, I will give letters of introduction to the men you approve *and send them with your gift to Jerusalem.*
>
> emphasis added

The support was not for the Pharisees, the Sadducees or even the impoverished community. It was for Jewish believers in Jerusalem.

I believe the bulk of Christian support for Israel should be directed to Jewish believers in the land first and foremost. These should be our primary relationships. Our blessing of the nation of Israel is best expressed when it is through the Messianic body in the land.

We also need to raise our voices in support of Jewish believers in the land whenever their rights are violated. Many Jews are deprived of their legal rights to make aliyah (to immigrate to Israel) when it is discovered they are Messianic. Loans and jobs are refused. Many endure verbal and, in some cases, physical attacks, while police turn the other way. They are looking to their brethren, true Believers, to speak out and stand with them in prayer.

The support of Jewish believers, particularly within the land of Israel, is an absolute must for those who claim to love the land and people of Israel.

8. Speak out against Replacement Theology.

On the other side of the spectrum, we have Replacement Theology. Again, Replacement Theology teaches that because Israel has been disobedient to God and rejected Jesus as the Messiah, the Church has now replaced the Jewish people as God's chosen people. Replacement Theology also says that the Jewish people no longer have any legitimate claim to the land. This theology renders the Jewish people and Israel irrelevant at best.

Replacement Theology and Dual Covenant Theology represent opposite ends of the spectrum, but both end with the same result: They keep the Gospel from reaching the Jewish people.

I also urge you who are reading this book to speak out against any form of Replacement Theology and try to help those who have been influenced by this demonic lie to understand that God does still love the Jewish people and has not rejected them, that Israel is part of His divine restoration and plan for the Last Days.

9. Embrace your Jewish roots.

Jesus was Jewish. He is not simply the Savior of the Gentiles, but was and is the Jewish Messiah who fulfilled the prophecies written hundreds of years before He was born. Furthermore, the first-century Church (ekklesia or "called-out ones") was made up entirely of Jewish people or proselytes to Judaism. These people never forsook the traditions of their fathers.

When the Gospel spread to the Gentiles, they came into what they understood to be a sect or distinctive group of Judaism. Although the council of Jerusalem (see Acts 15) made it clear that Gentiles do not have to become Jews in order to be saved, Paul taught that Gentile believers are wild branches that have been grafted into the natural olive branch, which is Israel (see Romans 11:17). As a wild olive branch that has been grafted in, your roots are now Jewish. You are a spiritual son or daughter of Abraham, and it is important that you understand and embrace your Jewish roots.

Christianity has evolved into a religious institution distinct from Judaism that has little, if anything, in common with the religion out of which it was born. But in reality, true New Testament faith is built upon the Torah and the prophets and better resembles the faith of the first-century believers. Many Christians view the Torah as legalism and bondage, when in fact, through relationship with God, we are enabled to go above and beyond the commandments of Torah because the law has been written in our hearts and on our minds (see Jeremiah 31:33).

If you invite a Jewish friend to your home to celebrate a Passover Seder, demonstrating how Yeshua is the Passover Lamb and the center of this observance, or if you invite that person to observe a Shabbat meal in your home and in their presence pray blessings over your children as instructed in Torah, then you are able to explain that the God you serve is the God of Israel. You can describe how the Jewish Messiah changed your life. You are honoring your roots, and you are provoking the Jewish people to jealousy.

I caution you, however, that your God-breathed love for Israel and the Jewish people be kept in balance. Be sure that your expression of your Jewish roots does not lead to legalism, a belief that Christians should be keeping the laws of Moses in detail and commanding others to do so, and that this somehow makes us holier or more righteous than other believers. This is patently unscriptural. We are saved by grace through faith alone (see Ephesians 2:8–9).

The Jews of the first century who put their faith in Yeshua never meant to start a religious movement that was separate and distinct from Judaism. The expectation was that the Jewish people, as a nation, would turn to Yeshua en masse, and for a while it seemed that was going to happen. The book of Acts records thousands coming to faith in a single day, and these early believers continued to worship in the Temple, circumcise their children and follow the Jewish dietary laws.

The apostle Paul went to the synagogue every Sabbath, even when he was on his missionary trips (see Acts 18:4, for example). It was only when opposition grew and Paul was no longer welcome in the synagogue that he went to the Gentiles. As the Gospel continued to spread among the Gentiles, what began as a Jewish movement eventually evolved into what became Christianity. In the years that followed, Jewish people were told they could not follow Yeshua and maintain their Jewish customs, traditions and practice. The two became incompatible.

As early as 150 years after the birth of Yeshua, Justin Martyr wrote to Trypho the Jew, telling him, "You can be a Jew or a Christian, but you can't be both." And that is pretty much how it has been. Jews who accepted Yeshua were expected to leave the Jewish culture behind and fit into the Christian Church. Only within the last hundred years or so has this begun to change as Jews who have come to faith in Yeshua have asked, "Why should I have to give up my cultural heritage?"

Why indeed? There is nothing un-Christian about a Jewish believer worshiping on the Sabbath or observing Passover or the other appointed days of Leviticus 23. Yet if you are a Gentile Christian, you can get in touch with your Jewish roots without wearing a skull cap and a *tallit* (prayer shawl). You don't have to *become* Jewish to appreciate your Jewish roots. The Bible says, "There is neither Jew nor Greek, slave nor free, male nor female, for you are all one in [the Messiah] Jesus" (Galatians 3:28). We are all one in Yeshua, yet we do not all have to start behaving one way. I am a man, and I act like a man. My wife is a woman, and she acts like a woman. But we do not differ in regard to our position in Messiah. Likewise, I am a Jew by birth, and in many ways I act like a Jew. Your heritage may be English, French, German or African. It is perfectly fine for each of us to be proud of our heritage and demonstrate that in our daily lives. God made us all the way we are.

The important thing is to remember that our Savior was and is Jewish. We owe the Jewish people a debt of gratitude for the many blessings that have come to us through them, most of all our Savior.

Bless God's Chosen People

These nine points are ways to fulfill God's call to bless the Jews, His chosen people. I encourage you to use these guidelines in your daily life to bless the Jewish people on a regular basis. If you do your best to love the Jewish people and pray for and support the nation of Israel, then you are blessing His people, and God says that you, in turn, will be blessed.

There is no question regarding God's Word on the blessing or cursing of Israel. And if we look at what happens to individuals and countries when they do either, we can see this promise of God being played out today before our very eyes. I will say it again: If a country blesses Israel, then that country will be blessed. But if a country curses (harms or does not support) Israel, then God will lift His hand of protection, and that country will be cursed; that is, the country will no longer come under the providential protection and hand of God.

In the United States, it would be prudent for our nation to recognize that God's continued blessing and protection over us is directly connected to our blessing and support of the Jewish people and the nation of Israel. May we be the world's strongest supporters of the nation of Israel.

As you stand up and be a conduit of blessing for Israel and the Jewish people, you are fulfilling an aspect of your end-time call—to provoke the Jewish people to jealousy and to bring His shalom to the land and people of Israel. In return, you will be blessed.

11

Jesus and the History of Israel

If you have ever been to the National Mall in Washington, D.C., then you are familiar with the Reflecting Pool between the Lincoln Memorial and the Washington Monument. On a bright summer's day, the reflection in that pool is so clear that it appears as if a building is down in the water. But of course, it is only a reflection.

I have discovered that the history of Israel is like looking into a reflection of Yeshua Himself, and vice versa. In other words, Yeshua's life parallels the history of Israel, and the history of Israel was relived through His life.

A Foreshadowing

The entire history of Israel was a foreshadowing of the life, death and atonement of the Messiah. Let me give you a few examples:

In Genesis, God called upon Abraham to sacrifice his only son, Isaac, as a test of faith. In obedience, Abraham took Isaac to a mountain. In answer to Isaac's question, "Where is the sacrifice?" Abraham made this statement in Genesis 22:8: "God himself will provide the lamb for the burnt offering, my son." Just as Abraham was ready to plunge the knife into Isaac, the Lord stopped him and provided a ram caught in the thicket as a substitute for the sacrifice.

This event foreshadows God's gift of His only begotten Son as a sacrifice for us. In fact, many scholars agree that Golgotha, the place of Yeshua's crucifixion (see Matthew 27:33), was the same spot where Abraham took Isaac to sacrifice him. This is more than just a coincidence. This is part of a divinely orchestrated plan.

Another interesting example to note is the life of Joseph. Joseph was the favorite son of his father and had a unique gifting and call. Out of jealousy and envy, his brothers despised and rejected him. Though they sold him into slavery and he was later imprisoned, Joseph ultimately was raised up by God to rule over his own brothers.

Yeshua's life parallels the life of Joseph. Like Joseph, Yeshua was despised and rejected by His own people. He was imprisoned but ultimately was raised up to rule over His people (see Isaiah 53:1–2, Psalm 2 and Matthew 27–28). It is also interesting to note that when Joseph's brothers first saw him, they did not recognize him because of his Egyptian appearance. He was simply changed beyond recognition. In the same way, the Jewish people fail to recognize Yeshua because He looks like Jesus Christ, God of the Christians. His appearance has been de-Judaized and replaced with foreign elements, such as light hair, fair skin, blue eyes and clothing that does not suggest His culture. When Joseph took his brothers into a room alone, they recognized him, possibly because he removed his Egyptian clothing, jewelry and makeup. Likewise, Yeshua's Jewish identity must be reestablished so He is seen not as Jesus Christ, the God of Christianity, but as Yeshua HaMashiach, the promised Messiah of Israel. It is then that the Jewish people will look upon Him whom they have pierced and mourn for Him as one mourns for an only child (see Zechariah 12:10), in the same way Joseph's brothers wailed as they recognized their brother.

A third example is seen in the children of Israel, who left their land to escape certain death from a terrible famine and journeyed to Egypt to seek safety. At the appointed time, God brought them out of Egypt and back to the land of their forefathers. In the same way, Yeshua lived out this part of Israel's history when His earthly father, Joseph, took Him and His mother to escape certain death at the hands of King Herod (see Genesis 42:1–47:12 and Matthew 2:13–18). And then when the time was right, the Lord instructed them to return to the land of Israel (see Hosea 11:1).

Furthermore, the Israelites passed through the waters of the Red Sea as they fled from the Egyptian army en route to the Promised Land. This event foreshadowed Yeshua's immersion (tefillah) in the waters of the Jordan at the start of His earthly ministry (see Matthew 3:13–17). And after they passed through those waters, the Israelites wandered in the wilderness for forty years before entering the Promised Land. Yeshua followed this same pattern by spending forty days in the wilderness after passing through the waters of mikvah (see Exodus 16:1–17:7 and Matthew 4:1–11).

After the Israelites left Egypt, Moses received the tablets of the law from God on the mountain (Mount Sinai). This is the foundational teaching of Judaism called the Torah, literally "instruction." The rabbis teach that the oral law (Talmud) was received by Moses on Mount Sinai as well. Likewise, the most important teaching recorded during Yeshua's earthly ministry is referred to as "The Sermon on the Mount" and was given on the Mount of Olives. Just as Israel *receives* the law on the mountain, Yeshua *reinterprets* the law on the mountain (see Exodus 19:1–23 and Matthew 5–7).

After Moses was given the Torah, we are told that his face shone with the glory of God (see Exodus 34:29–35). In the same way, Yeshua embodied the glory of God on the Mount of Transfiguration as Matthew records in chapter 17, verse 2: "His face shone like the sun, and his clothes became as white as the light."

Scripture contains many other examples, including, of course, the whole sacrificial system, which provided the basis of understanding for Yeshua's atoning death. Hebrews 10:1 tells us that those things that came before (the Torah and the Prophets) were foreshadows of that which was to come.

The Feasts

Yeshua's life was also mirrored in the seven *moadim* (appointed times, or festivals, feasts) of the biblical calendar found in Leviticus 23.

The first feast mentioned is the Shabbat, a weekly celebration. It is followed by six feasts (seven, depending on whether or not you separate Passover and the Feast of Unleavened Bread, but we will treat these as one). These six feasts are broken into two groups: the three Spring Feasts and the three Fall Feasts. The three Spring Feasts—the Passover (including the Feast of Unleavened Bread), First Fruits and Shavuot (Pentecost), are directly connected to the First Coming of Messiah—His life, atoning death at Calvary and the outpouring of His Spirit on the first believers assembled in Jerusalem.

There is then a significant gap in time between those and the three Feasts that follow: Rosh Hashanah (Trumpets), Yom Kippur (Day of Atonement) and Sukkot (Tabernacles). The gap itself is significant, as it indicates a period of time between the first three and the last three, and each of these last three are directly connected to Yeshua's physical return to this earth (Second Coming) and the establishment of His millennial reign.

What is interesting to note is that all these festivals on the Jewish calendar include some dimension of Messianic hope. In other words, they have a connection to the coming of the Messiah. Paul reiterates this in the New Testament when he declares:

> Therefore do not let anyone judge you by what you eat or drink, or with regard to a religious festival, a New Moon celebration or a Sabbath day. These are a shadow of the things that were to come; the reality, however, is found in [Messiah].
>
> Colossians 2:16–17

Let's look at each appointed moadim (festival) in greater detail:

Passover and the Feast of Unleavened Bread

Passover is the watershed event in Jewish history. It is probably the Jewish holiday most familiar to non-Jews. Biblically, it marks the beginning of the New Year (*Aviv* or *Nisan*). Of all the holidays in Leviticus 23, Passover has the clearest connection to the sacrificial death of the Messiah.

The story is a classic. Moses was sent by God to Pharaoh to free the Israelites, who had become slaves in Egypt and had been crying out for deliverance for more than four hundred years. With a mighty hand and outstretched arm, God spoke through Moses to "Let My people go!" When Pharaoh refused to listen, God sent ten plagues on the land of Egypt.

After the first nine plagues, Pharaoh's heart remained hardened, so God released the tenth and most severe of all the plagues—the death of the firstborn in each family. To avert this judgment on the Israelites, God instructed Moses that every Hebrew family was to sacrifice a lamb without blemish. After the lamb had been killed, some of its blood was to be placed on the top and two sides of the door frames of their homes. The people were then to enter through the bloodstained door and eat the meal of the lamb, which included bitter herbs and unleavened bread, called *matzo*.

At midnight the Lord passed through Egypt and killed the firstborn child of every household. He *passed over*, however, the households that had blood on the doors, sparing the firstborn of those families. The blood of the lamb saved them from death and eventually brought the Israelites their freedom, as Pharaoh finally relented. The Passover story in Exodus 12 is a detailed prototype of the Lamb of God, who overcame death and takes away the sins of the world.

The Passover was a foreshadowing of the Gospel, and Yeshua's atonement fulfills the Passover in detail:

1. **Everyone required a lamb.** The Bible tells us that all have sinned and come short of God's righteous standard. Just as each Israelite family had to be covered by the blood, so do we as believers in Yeshua.

2. **The whole congregation of Israel was to kill the lamb.** For almost two thousand years, the Jews have been blamed for killing Jesus. This has led to a legacy of hatred and anti-Semitism. It was all of us, however—the whole house, Christian and Jew, Arab and Muslim, atheist and agnostic—who were responsible for His death. He laid down His life for all of us. It was our sin—yours and mine—that required the Lamb to die.

3. **The lamb was to be without blemish.** Yeshua, the Lamb of God who took away the sins of the world, was without flaw (in other words, sin). "For you know that it was

not with perishable things such as silver or gold that you were redeemed from the empty way of life handed down to you from your forefathers, but with the precious blood of Christ, a lamb without blemish or defect" (1 Peter 1:18–19).

4. **The children of Israel entered through the blood-covered door into safety and divine protection.** It was this door to which Yeshua was referring when He said, "I am the door. If anyone enters by Me, he will be saved" (see John 10:9).

5. **The lamb was to be roasted with fire, which is symbolic of judgment.** In Yeshua's atoning death, we are told that God placed upon Him the sins of us all. "God made him who had no sin to be sin for us, so that in him we might become the righteousness of God" (2 Corinthians 5:21).

6. **The children of Israel were to eat the roasted lamb as a fellowship meal** prescribed in Genesis 12. This is what Yeshua referred to when He said, "You must eat My body and drink My blood." In addition, the Passover meal was to be fully eaten; none of it was to remain until morning. Likewise, Yeshua's body was removed from the tree of execution before sunset (the beginning of Shabbat) and buried in the tomb; the Passover Lamb did not remain until morning.

7. **Not a bone of the Passover lamb was to be broken** (see Exodus 12:46). John clearly is referring to this requirement when he parallels Yeshua as the Lamb when he says in John 19:32–33 that they broke the legs of the first man who had been crucified with Yeshua, and then those of the other. But when they came to Yeshua, they saw that He was already dead and did not break His legs.

8. **The matzo represented His body.** The matzo used in the first Passover meal—and in every Passover meal

since—foreshadowed Yeshua. This bread made without yeast represented the hasty departure of the Israelites from Egypt. It is flat because it has no yeast, which is symbolic of sin. It also is striped and pierced. Yeshua's body was broken for us. He was without sin. He was pierced for our transgressions, and by His stripes we were healed (see Isaiah 53:5).

9. **The wine represented His shed blood.** At Yeshua's final Passover meal on earth, the Last Passover Supper, He raised the cup of wine and prayed over it the traditional Hebrew prayer: *"Baruch atah ADONAI, Eloheynu Melech ha'olam, borey p'ri ha'gafen"* ("Blessed are You, O Lord, our God, King of the Universe, who creates the fruit of the vine"). He was actually lifting the "The Third Cup," traditionally known as the Cup of Redemption. This redemption originally commemorated the redemption out of Egypt but is now fulfilled in Yeshua's shed blood, which brings us redemption from sin and entrance into the Promised Land of eternal life.

Clearly, Yeshua fulfills the Passover lamb of Exodus 12 in great detail.

The Feast of Firstfruits

This feast, or appointed day, is described in Leviticus 23:9–14. It commemorated the barley harvest—the first harvest of the season. Yeshua directly fulfills this event by becoming the firstfruits of life from the dead (see Acts 6:23).

In Judaism today, Firstfruits is somewhat of a parenthetical observance. But for we who are followers of the Messiah, this is the single most important event of our faith—the resurrection of the Messiah. The apostle Paul makes it clear that the resurrection provides the foundation for our faith and that without the Messiah's resurrection from the dead, our faith is in vain.

> But Christ has indeed been raised from the dead, the firstfruits of those who have fallen asleep. For since death came through a man, the resurrection of the dead comes also through a man. For as in Adam all die, so in Christ all will be made alive. But each in his own turn: Christ, the firstfruits; then, when he comes, those who belong to him.
>
> 1 Corinthians 15:20–23

Shavuot (The Feast of Weeks/Pentecost)

Shavuot is the final harvest of the spring agricultural cycle. *Shavuot* is derived from the Hebrew word *sheva*, meaning "seven." It refers to "seven periods of seven," or 49 days. On the fiftieth day, we celebrate the great wheat harvest. The Greek word for the celebration is *Pentecost*, derived from the word *pente*, meaning "five" or "fifty." It is also called the Feast of Weeks because it takes place seven weeks and one day after the Feast of Firstfruits. In Leviticus, God says:

> From the day after the Sabbath, the day you brought the sheaf of the wave offering, count off seven full weeks. Count off fifty days up to the day after the seventh Sabbath, and then present an offering of new grain to the LORD.
>
> Leviticus 23:15–16

According to the ancient rabbis, it was on Shavuot that Moses received the Law on Mount Sinai. Again, this festival was a shadow of that which would come. We know from the parable of the wheat and tares (see Matthew 13:24–30) that wheat represents souls. The Law was a shadow of that which was to come; it is on Shavuot that the Spirit is now poured out on those gathered in the Temple for this pilgrimage feast and three thousand Jews are saved. Just as Shavuot celebrated the literal wheat harvest, we now celebrate the first harvest of souls into the Kingdom of God, the body of Messiah. Shavuot marks the birth of the first Church, or as I prefer to call it, the Messianic community.

The Spring Feasts, therefore, are directly connected to the First Coming of the Messiah almost two thousand years ago. He fulfills Passover as the Lamb of God who takes away the sins of the world and is resurrected on First Fruits as the first fruits of life from the dead, and the Spirit of God is poured out on Shavuot, bringing in the first harvest of souls into God's Kingdom.

The next three feasts take place following a significant gap in time. They are known as the Fall Feasts and will be fulfilled in the last days, immediately preceding the actual return of Yeshua and the establishment of His millennial Kingdom here on earth. Let's take a closer look these.

Rosh Hashanah (The Feast of Trumpets)

The term *Rosh Hashanah* literally means "head of the year" in Hebrew. Today in Judaism, it is considered a high holiday—a significant event—the Jewish New Year. According to the rabbis, God began creating the world on the first day of the seventh month, so Rosh Hashanah is a commemoration of creation. This is a later development of rabbinic Judaism, however, and is not the original name for this feast. In the Torah, the feast is named *Yom Teru'ah*, or the "feast of shofars or blowing (a day of sounding)."

The actual biblical first month of the year was the month of Nisan or Aviv, when Passover actually took place. Little is said about the Feast of Trumpets in Leviticus 23. We are simply told that the first day of the seventh month is to be a day of rest commemorated with trumpet, or shofar, blasts.

> The LORD said to Moses, "Say to the Israelites: 'On the first day of the seventh month you are to have a day of rest, a sacred assembly commemorated with trumpet blasts. Do no regular work, but present an offering made to the LORD by fire.'"
>
> Leviticus 23:23–25

The blowing of the shofar prophetically has great significance. In ancient Israel, a shofar was blown for two important purposes. One was to announce a call to sacred assembly and gather together the people for worship. The second was to sound an alarm to warn the people of an impending attack from an invading army. According to the tradition of the rabbis, a third purpose for blowing the shofar was to confound and confuse the enemy, as seen in Judges 7, where Gideon and his army of three hundred men used shofars to confuse and frighten the Midianites. In addition, in the book of Joshua, the walls of Jericho tumbled down as a result of the shofar blasts.

The Feast of Trumpets takes place during the month of Elul (the seventh month) and is a time of repentance and preparation. Elul is an acronym of "*Ani l'dodi v'dodi li*," or "I am my Beloved's and my Beloved is mine," a quote from the Song of Songs (Song of Solomon 6:3). In Aramaic, the word *Elul* means "search," which is appropriate, because this is a season when we are to search our hearts before God. It is followed by what is known in Judaism as "The Days of Awe," leading up to Yom Kippur, the day of repentance.

The prophetic symbolism of the Feast of Trumpets is immense. I am certain that this feast is directly fulfilled in the last days, and we are entering that period now.

Revelation 8 speaks of seven trumpet blasts that release the judgments of God upon the earth. They directly parallel the plagues of Egypt before the Exodus. To read them is horrifying. We sing the popular song, "Blow the Trumpet in Zion" with great gusto, as if we are proclaiming the blessings and victory of God, something we should look forward to with great expectation and excitement. But in fact, this song is talking about the shofar blast warning the earth to prepare for disaster. These are the blasts signaling doom, not blessing. But there is also good news for those of us who know the Lord.

Another shofar is mentioned, and this one is to announce a divine gathering:

> For the Lord himself will come down from heaven, with a loud command, with the voice of the archangel and with the *trumpet call of God*, and the dead in Christ will rise first. After that, we who are still alive and are left will be caught up with them in the clouds to meet the Lord in the air. And so we will be with the Lord forever. Therefore encourage each other with these words.
>
> 1 Thessalonians 4:16–18, emphasis added

I am not going to get into a discussion of the Rapture here, and tell you whether or not I believe in a pre-, mid- or post-Rapture. Strong cases can be made for each of these three positions. Suffice it to say, for we who know God and are in right standing with Him, the shofar blast is a divine summons to meet the Lord in the air and reign with Him forever. The feast of Yom Teru'ah prophetically points to these end-time events.

Yom Kippur

Ten days following Rosh Hashanah comes Yom Kippur or Yom Teru'ah, or the "Day of Atonement"—the holiest day of the Jewish year. Whereas the other moadim (appointed days or festivals) are joyous occasions that include eating and celebrating, Yom Kippur is a solemn day of acknowledging our sins and shortcomings before God and seeking His forgiveness and mercy.

On Yom Kippur, Jewish people all over the world gather together in places of worship to recite the traditional liturgy to petition God for forgiveness and mercy. Many fast and pray, yet they have no understanding of the need for a sacrificial atonement that requires the shedding of blood. With the destruction of the Temple in AD 70, rabbinic Judaism replaced the requirement for sacrifice and the shedding of blood for atonement with a new system, which included simple acts of prayer, repentance and good deeds to atone for sin. This is not, however, a biblically based view, which requires blood sacrifice for the atoning of our souls (see Leviticus 17:11).

The biblical commands for the Day of Atonement are found in Leviticus 23:

> The LORD said to Moses, "The tenth day of this seventh month is the Day of Atonement. Hold a sacred assembly and deny yourselves, and present an offering made to the LORD by fire. Do no work on that day, because it is the Day of Atonement, when atonement is made for you before the LORD your God. Anyone who does not deny himself on that day must be cut off from his people. I will destroy from among his people anyone who does any work on that day. You shall do no work at all. This is to be a lasting ordinance for the generations to come, wherever you live. It is a Sabbath of rest for you, and you must deny yourselves. From the evening of the ninth day of the month until the following evening you are to observe your Sabbath."
>
> Leviticus 23:26–32

This is traditionally understood as a day of fasting and repentance. It was the only time that the High Priest could enter the

Holy of Holies, first in the Tabernacle and later in the Temple, not only to atone for his sins and the sins of his family, but for the entire nation.

On this day, two flawless goats would be be brought to the Temple. One would be chosen for the sacrifice. The high priest of Israel would lay his hands on the other, symbolically placing the sins of the entire nation on it. While the first was sacrificed, the second would be driven into the wilderness, symbolically carrying the nation's sins far away from the people.

The New Testament book of Hebrews provides further insight into Yom Kippur, revealing that Yeshua, our High Priest, made atonement, but not with the hands of man. Nor did He enter the physical Holy of Holies, but actually brought His atoning blood to the Holy of Holies in the heavenly Tabernacle. This is a marvelous fulfillment of the priesthood of Melchizedek making atonement for our sins once and for all (see Hebrews 8–10). So, in part, Yeshua prophetically fulfilled Yom Kippur with the shedding of His blood and delivering this atonement to His Father in heaven. As He was led out of the city for crucifixion, He also fulfilled the requirement of the scapegoat, which was led out into the wilderness. But this is only a partial fulfillment. The best way to understand the word *fulfill* is to reverse the syllables: "fill full."

The cup of Yom Kippur is not yet filled to fullness but will be filled to overflowing upon His return. After the blowing of the shofar as both a warning to the earth that leads to the outpouring of God's judgments and the shofar blast that summons us to meet Him in the air, we will see a national awakening take place with Israel as they recognize the One whom they have pierced as their Messiah:

> I will pour out on the house of David and the inhabitants of Jerusalem a spirit of grace and supplication. They will look on me, the one they have pierced, and they will mourn for him as

one mourns for an only child, and grieve bitterly for him as one grieves for a firstborn son.

Zechariah 12:10

And we are then told in Zechariah 13:1, "On that day a fountain will be opened to the house of David and the inhabitants of Jerusalem, to cleanse them from sin and impurity."

The clarity of this prophecy is astounding! It declares in detail the day when the Jewish people, and specifically the inhabitants of a Jerusalem under Jewish control, recognize that Jesus, whom they previously understood to be the God of the Christians and whom they denied since the days of their ancestors some two thousand years ago, is in fact Yeshua, the promised Messiah of Israel.

As a response to this revelation, they will enter into true repentance and mourning as was commanded of them in Torah during Yom Kippur. This will be the "filling full" of this holy day. It is also a direct fulfillment of Yeshua's declaration as He wept over Jerusalem, saying:

O Jerusalem, Jerusalem, you who kill the prophets and stone those sent to you, how often I have longed to gather your children together, as a hen gathers her chicks under her wings, but you were not willing. Look, your house is left to you desolate. For I tell you, you will not see me again until you say, "Blessed is he who comes in the name of the Lord."

Matthew 23:37–39

What a glorious day that will be when those who were first promised the New Covenant finally accept Yeshua as their Messiah, and as God promised in Jeremiah 31:34, "They all shall know Me, from the least of them to the greatest of them. . . . For I will forgive their iniquity, and their sin I will remember no more" (NKJV). This end-time event, in my opinion, is the most significant event that must take place before Yeshua can dwell on this earth and establish His millennial reign for a thousand years.

This is exactly what Paul meant when he stated in Romans 11:25–26, that when the blindness comes off of the eyes of the Jewish people, "all Israel shall be saved." Notice that it is immediately following this widespread Jewish acceptance of Jesus as their Messiah that the Deliverer will then return to Zion (verse 26).

Sukkot

The third and final Fall Feast that will see its fulfillment in Messiah's return is Sukkot, also known as the Feast of Tabernacles, the Feast of Booths, or the Feast of Ingathering. Sukkot, which begins five days after Yom Kippur, is a seven-day period when the Jewish people remember God's faithfulness and provision through their forty-year period of wandering in the desert after the Exodus. Leviticus 23:33–43 has a lot to say about this appointed day.

This festival points to Yeshua in so many ways. First, it is a celebration of the divine provision of manna that God provided in the wilderness. In John 6:48–51, Jesus refers to Himself as the Bread of Life who feeds those who come to Him:

> I am the Bread of Life. Your forefathers ate the manna in the desert, yet they died. But here is the Bread that comes down from heaven, which a man may eat and not die. I am the Living Bread that came down from heaven. If anyone eats of this Bread, he will live forever. This Bread is My flesh, which I will give for the life of the world.
>
> John 6:48–51

Yeshua directly refers to Himself as the fulfillment of this manna. In the wilderness, the manna sustained them physically, but Yeshua provides the manna that will sustain us spiritually for life everlasting.

Sukkot reminds us of the transience of life and the need for God's guidance. Just as the Israelites were led by the pillar of fire by night and the cloud by day, we also are sojourners on this earth who must move with God's presence. We are not citizens of America, Canada, the UK or any other country where you may hold a passport; we are citizens of heaven. Our time on this earth is but for a short season, and we must fulfill our destiny. Just as the children of Israel moved when the Lord's Spirit moved, we must be willing to do the same.

Every day during Sukkot, a water ceremony called *Nisuach HaMayim* was carried out. The High Priest and his assistant would draw water from the Pool of Siloam and pour out water and wine onto the altar of the Temple as the people sang, "With joy you will draw water from the wells of salvation" (Isaiah 12:3). The word used here for *salvation* is the name for Jesus, *Yeshua*.

It was most likely during this ceremony that Yeshua stood up and cried out in a loud voice, "If anyone is thirsty, let him come to me and drink. Whoever believes in me, as the Scripture has said, streams of living water will flow from within him" (John 7:37–38).

Another significant event of Sukkot is related to branches: "On the first day you are to take choice fruit from the trees, and palm fronds, leafy branches and poplars, and rejoice before the LORD your God for seven days" (Leviticus 23:40). This is connected to Psalm 118, known as the great *hallel*, the Hebrew word for "praise," and was directly tied to Messianic expectation. And this was the very thing the Jewish inhabitants of Jerusalem did when Jesus entered Jerusalem with His disciples. They waved branches, called *lulavs*, and proclaimed, "Blessed is he who comes in the name of the Lord!" (Matthew 21:9).

Not only does Psalm 118 welcome the Messiah, but it also prophetically predicts the rejection of Yeshua. Before the great declaration *"Baruch haba b'shem Adonai"* ("Blessed is he who comes in the name of the Lord") (verse 22), this passage reveals that the stone the builders rejected would become the cornerstone. That is exactly what Yeshua was and is, and yet the Jewish people will continue to reject that cornerstone until a set time in history. I believe we are entering into the set time now.

Sukkot is also an agricultural feast celebrating the final gathering of the harvest for the year. The final fulfillment of Sukkot will be what Matthew describes: "And He will send His angels with a great sound of a trumpet, and they will gather together His elect from the four winds, from one end of heaven to the other" (Matthew 24:31, NKJV).

While this also could be tied to the Feast of Trumpets, I believe this verse refers to the fulfillment of Sukkot, the final gathering of God's elect together in the establishment of His millennial Kingdom, where He will reign physically on this earth for a thousand-year period.

On the Threshold of the Fall Feasts

The prophets of the Old Testament wrote much about the millennial Kingdom and the prophetic fulfillment of these moadim. They were looking toward the day when the Messiah would take His throne in Jerusalem and assume His rightful position as King of kings and Lord of lords—both High Priest and King. I believe that we are on the threshold of the prophetic fulfillment of the Fall Feasts.

It saddens me to think that every year, millions of my Jewish brethren all over the world celebrate these appointed days that point so clearly to their Messiah, and yet they look through veiled eyes. Like Paul, my heart's desire for Israel is that they might be saved.

I also pray that you will play a role in bringing about this glorious promised day of Israel's redemption. I encourage you to be a light to those Jewish people in your life. They are not there by accident.

My final encouragement to you as I close this chapter is to fulfill your destiny and purpose for your remaining time here on this earth. The time is truly short. The laborers are few. The harvest is ripe. And we must be about the work of Him who sent us while it is yet day, for night will come when no man can work (see John 9:4).

12

The Best Is Yet to Come

I am often asked by well-meaning viewers of my television program, *Jewish Voice with Jonathan Bernis*, why I spend so much time talking about end-time prophecy. These questions remind me of a remark a college professor wrote on a paper I once submitted on end-time prophecy. He said that although he "found my paper intriguing, we need to focus on the first advent, rather than the second."

Yes, Yeshua's First Coming is vitally important and foundational, as His death at Calvary paved the way for all of us to receive salvation. But my answer to that professor and to everyone else who asks me this question is that understanding end-time prophecy should make God's people better witnesses to those who need to hear the message of God's love.

Daniel 12

In Daniel 12, the prophet Daniel wrote a number of astounding statements under the inspiration of the Holy Spirit. One of these says, "And many of those who sleep in the dust of the earth shall awake, some to everlasting life, some to shame and everlasting contempt" (Daniel 12:2).

I believe this is an Old Testament reference to the reality of heaven and hell. Many Jewish people argue that there is nothing in their Scriptures that mentions heaven or hell, but I would disagree. "Shame and everlasting contempt" sure sound like hell to me. I do not even want to imagine an eternity of regretting the wrong decisions and actions I have taken in this life, nor do I want to spend an eternity of no more hope—complete and utter separation from God.

Likewise, everlasting life, as I understand it, is true joy, peace and fulfillment. It is life in the presence of God, experiencing His presence in a way that is beyond anything we have experienced in this life. It is the gift of eternal life that Jesus spoke of so often during His time on earth.

Daniel 12:3 then says, "Those who are wise shall shine like the brightness of the firmament, and those who turn many to righteousness like the stars forever and ever." In the words that follow, the Lord tells Daniel to "seal the words of the scroll until the time of the end." He then shares with us an amazing revelation that in the last days, "many shall run to and fro, and knowledge shall be increased" (KJV).

Running "to and fro" indicates an increase in travel, and the increase of knowledge is clearly related to the technological boom. Both of these are happening before our very eyes. Only a hundred years ago a trip to Europe required traveling by ocean liner, which took a minimum of five days. Today, planes take us to every continent in the world in only hours. Information is available at our fingertips in a matter of seconds. The advancements we are seeing today in travel and technology are like no other time in human history. To imagine that Daniel saw all this more than 2,500 years ago is nothing short of mind-boggling!

Daniel 12 gives a specific revelation about the end times: They would arrive during a boom in technology and travel. That is exactly the time in which we now live!

Furthermore, the revelation concerning the last days was sealed by God until a set time—a time I believe we have entered. The seal is now broken, the fullness of time has come, and knowledge concerning the last days is flowing to God's people. It is certainly God's will for His people to understand these mysteries that were previously hidden because they are directly connected to our effectiveness in turning many to righteousness.

Acts 3: Messiah Is Waiting

Acts 3, which I mentioned earlier, offers another revelation that is critical to understanding what must happen before Jesus returns. Peter proclaims to the people of Israel:

> Repent, then, and turn to God, so that your sins may be wiped out, that times of refreshing may come from the Lord, and that he may send the [Messiah], who has been appointed for you—even Yeshua. He must remain in heaven until the time comes for God to restore everything, as he promised long ago through his holy prophets.
>
> Acts 3:19–21

An important truth is being revealed here! The Messiah [Jesus] is actually waiting in heaven. What is He waiting for? He is waiting for God's appointed people to intersect with God's appointed time and fulfill the restoration prophesied in the Word of God.

This prophesied restoration includes the salvation of Israel, as well as the Church's coming into its destined fullness (see Romans 11:25)—a fullness that includes returning to the Jewish roots of the faith, understanding God's faithfulness to and His plan for Israel, restoring holiness and truth, and the same dimension of God's power experienced by the first believers in Jerusalem.

This is all happening now. As we have discussed, more Jews believe in Jesus today than at any time in history, likely including the first century. Just forty years ago, only a handful of Messianic Jewish congregations existed in America and Israel. Today more than 300 Messianic Jewish congregations are active in America and more than a hundred in Israel. Just about every city in the world that has a major Jewish population, especially in Europe and the former Soviet Union, now has Messianic Jewish congregations. And we are witnessing an incredible hunger and interest among Christians to truly understand the Jewish roots of their faith, as well as an increased love and support for Israel and the Jewish people. Overwhelmingly today, Christians want to bless Israel and the Jewish people.

What Should We Then Do?

I used to think how great it would have been to have lived during the time of Jesus—to have watched Him perform all those miracles and teach those powerful messages. But the more I understand the day in which we live, the more grateful I am that I was born at this time, in this season. Each day we draw one day closer to the return of the Messiah to the earth. But until that time arrives, how should we live?

1. Live like there is no tomorrow.

Do you ever get out of bed in the morning and think, *This could be my last day on earth?* We need to live this way, as though this was the last day of our lives! God wants us to understand the mysteries He is revealing in this set time in history. He wants us to live in expectation: always watching, always waiting with anticipation.

2. Be vigilant: Watch and pray.

Jesus told us that His return will catch the world by surprise, that He will come like a "thief in the night" (1 Thessalonians 5:2). He will come when the world least expects Him. Those who love Him, however, are not to be caught off guard. Again, this is why I believe understanding the times in which we live are imperative. Over and over again, God says, "I do not want you to be ignorant of this mystery." He wants us to be sober. He wants us to be vigilant. He does not want these events to catch us by surprise. We are to watch and pray.

3. Occupy until He comes.

God does not want us—or *you*—to disengage, to retreat to the mountains and isolate ourselves, waiting out the time until He returns. The Bible is clear that we are to "occupy" until He comes (see Luke 19:13, KJV). This means that we are to remain active in all realms of society. We must make our voices known. We must carry out God's will through our lives until it is no longer possible to do so. We must be about the work of the Father while it is day, for night will come when no man can work (see John 9:4).

4. Let your light shine.

We are to let our light shine amidst a world that grows darker by the day. I do not agree with those who teach that Jesus can return only when we have successfully uprooted the kingdom of darkness and prevailed in establishing God's rule over the entire earth. This is not reality. The reality is that the world is spiraling into moral decay. One would have to be blind to ignore the increased activity of Satan and his hordes, and the resulting godlessness. The world is getting darker and darker—not brighter and brighter.

Yet as the world gets darker, it is God's will that His people, the Body of Messiah, grow brighter and brighter. As this happens, the lines of separation will be delineated more than ever before. True followers of Messiah will come out from among the world and will grow hungrier and hungrier for holiness, sanctification and the power of God. We will eventually return to a day when God is so manifest among His people that even our very shadows will heal the sick (see Acts 5:15). We are to walk close to the Lord so those around us will see in us the fruits of the Spirit, the peace that passes all understanding and the strong sense of destiny and purpose that drives our lives. They must see that we are here with a mission and that we remain unmoved through the various crises now coming upon the world. When all they have is uncertainty and fear, they must see in us a hope and expectation—and even excitement—for what lies ahead. This will draw them to us to find out what we have that they don't.

5. Do not worry about what is to come.

You may be worried about what is ahead. Will we experience economic collapse? What will happen to our loved ones who are not yet saved? I understand this concern, as I am still praying for the majority of my family who are not yet believers in their Messiah. The decisions we make in this life determine where we spend eternity, and it is devastating to think that people we love may miss out on the joys that lie ahead for those who love God. Yet God calls us to take no thought about tomorrow but to be about the Father's business today.

Can you imagine the foolishness of a football player whose team was about to win the Super Bowl but who was distressed and worried that the game clock was winding down? It would be ridiculous. The same is true for us. Why spend time worrying about what is ahead? The game has been won! Our victory is already won! The end of the story has already been written, and in the end we win! We just need to live out that victory.

We can focus so much time on the judgment and wrath that are to come that we miss the true messages:

- "No weapon formed against us will prosper" (Isaiah 54:17).
- "Greater is he that is in us than he that is in the world" (1 John 4:4).
- "We are more than conquerors through him who loves us" (Romans 8:37).

In the end, the whole world will be full of the knowledge of the Lord, and God Himself will wipe away every tear from the eyes of His people. Yeshua will bring this about when He sets up His earthly Kingdom. Our job is simply to endure and to fulfill our destinies until His return.

The Harvest Is Ready

I do not know who the Antichrist is, nor do I fully understand the mark of the beast and exactly what it represents or how it will come to pass. I do not know in detail how the scenario with Israel and the Islamic nations that are committed to her demise will ultimately play out. I do not know whether a rapture will be pre-, mid- or post-Tribulation. In all this I defer to others who have more expertise in those areas than I.

What I can tell you with confidence is that we are in the last days and in the end, God's plan for the redemption of Israel will be fulfilled in detail. What you do with this knowledge is absolutely imperative! God's desire is that you be an effective co-worker with Him in bringing to pass His promised last days revival and restoration, not only for Israel and the Jewish people but for the world.

So how will you spend your time in these final days ahead? God is looking for those who, like Isaiah, will say, "*Hineini*," "Here am I. Send me!" when He calls. Will you choose to help reach out and pray for your Jewish brothers and sisters until they come into a full knowledge of their Messiah? For if their rejection brought reconciliation to the world, what will their acceptance be but life from the dead? Time is short. The harvest is ready.

I have one ultimate desire in life. When I meet Yeshua upon His return—or should He tarry, when I pass from this life—I want to look into those eyes of love and compassion and hear Him say to me, "Good and faithful servant, come and enter My rest." This is my prayer for you, that you also will hear those words after being faithful to accomplish all that God has for you while you remain on this earth. May you fulfill your destiny and accomplish all He has for you to do in this life.

Notes

Chapter 1: What If Everything You Have Been Told about the Last Days Is Wrong?

1. "An Encyclopedia of Claims, Frauds, and Hoaxes of the Occult and Supernatural," James Randi Educational Foundation, http://www.randi.org/encyclopedia/appendix3.html.

2. "A Brief History of the Apocalypse," a site for failed doomsday prophecy, 1999–2011, Chris Nelson, http://www.abhota.info/end1.htm.

3. Michael Stifel, Wikipedia, http://en.wikipedia.org/wiki/Michael_Stifel.

4. John Napier, Wikipedia, http://en.wikipedia.org/wiki/John_Napier.

5. Richard G. Kyle, *The Last Days Are Here Again: A History of the End Times* (Grand Rapids, Mich.: Baker Books, 1998), 78–79.

6. George R. Knight, *Millennial Fever and the End of the World* (Boise, Idaho: Pacific Press, 1993), 222–223.

7. Edgar C. Whisenant, Wikipedia, http://en.wikipedia.org/wiki/Edgar_C._Whisenant.

Chapter 2: Why Satan Hates the Jews

1. Michael L. Brown, *Our Hands Are Stained with Blood: The Tragic Story of the "Church" and the Jewish People* (Shippensburg, Penn.: Destiny Image Publishers, Inc., 1992), 77–78.

2. Zionist Organization, *Die Judenpogrome in Russland*, 2 vols. (1909); Dubnow, Hist Russ, 3 (1920), index; *Yevreyskoye istorikoetnograficheskoye obshchestvo, Materialy dlyya istorii anti-yevreyskikh pogromov v Russii*, 2 vols. (1919–1923).

3. Adolf Eichmann, Wikipedia, http://en.wikipedia.org/wiki/Adolf_Eichmann.

Chapter 3: Aliyah: The Return of the Jews

1. Nathan Katz and Ellen S. Goldberg, "The Last Jews in India and Burma," *The Jerusalem Letter* (Jerusalem, Israel: Jerusalem Center for Public Affairs, No. 101, 15 April 1988), http://jcpa.org/jl/jl101.htm.

Chapter 4: Something Is Happening among the Jewish People

1. *Encyclopaedia Britannica*, 11th ed., s.v. "Johann August Wilhelm Neander."

2. David Van Biema, "10 Ideas That Are Changing the World," *Time*, March 24, 2008, 60.

3. Bob Dylan, "The Times They Are A-Changin'," recorded October 24, 1963, on *The Times They Are A-Changin'*, Columbia, CCC 124128615, LP.

Chapter 5: The Gospel to the Nations

1. Daniel Gruber, *The Church and the Jews: The Biblical Relationship* (Hanover, N.H.: Elijah Publishing, 2001), 30.

2. Alan Torres, "Replacement Theology," http://www.biblicist.org/bible/replace.shtml.

3. Raul Hilberg, *The Destruction of the European Jews* (New York: Holmes and Meier, 1985), 5.

4. Stephen Yulish, "Why Does Satan Hate Israel?," Prophecy Forum Website Ministries, accessed July 25, 2012, http://prophecyforum.com/yulish/satan.html.

Chapter 6: The Mystery of the Two Messiahs

1. "Rabbi Reveals Name of the Messiah," *Israel Today*, Monday, April 30, 2007, http://www.israeltoday.co.il//default.aspx?tabid=item&idx=1347.

2. Ibid.

3. Ibid.

4. "Authority in Deciding the Halakhah," Commentary on Deuteronomy 17:2–11, *Encyclopaedia Judaica,* vol. 3, AHN-AZ (Jerusalem, Israel: Keter Publishing House), 907.

5. Nadav Shragai, "Ex-chief Rabbi Opposes New Moves to Visit Temple Mount," Haaretz.com, May 16, 2007, http://www.haaretz.com/news/ex-chief-rabbi-opposes-new-moves-to-visit-temple-mount-1.220709.

6. Babylonian Talmud, Sanhedrin 98a.

7. Josh McDowell, *Evidence That Demands a Verdict* (San Bernardino, Calif.: Campus Crusade for Christ, 1972), 175.

8. Flavius Josephus, "From the Banishment of Archelaus to the Departure of the Jews from Babylon," *The Antiquities of the Jews, Complete Works,* book 18, trans. William Whiston (Grand Rapids, Mich.: Kregel, 1960), 379.

9. JewishEncyclopedia.com, s.v. "Martyrs, the Ten," accessed August 23, 2012, http://www.jewishencyclopedia.com/articles/10447-martyrs-the-ten.

10. *JewishEncyclopedia.com,* s.v. "Shabbethai Zebi B. Mordecai," accessed August 23, 2012, JewishEncyclopedia.com, http://www.jewishencyclopedia.com/articles/13480-shabbethai-zebi-b-mordecai.

11. Ibid.

12. Sue Fishkoff, *The Rebbe's Army: Inside the World of Chabad-Lubavitch* (New York: Schocken Books, 2003), 66–87.

Chapter 7: Are "The Times of the Gentiles" at an End?

1. Flavius Josephus, "War of the Jews," *The Antiquities of the Jews, Complete Works,* book 7, trans. William Whiston (Grand Rapids, Mich.: Kregel, 1960), 589.

2. "Aelia Capitolina: Judaism Expelled," GoJerusalem.com, accessed August 23, 2012, www.gojerusalem.com/article_520/Aelia-Capitolina-Judaism-Expelled.

3. *Encyclopedia Judaica,* s.v. "Bar Kokhba."

4. Rabbi Ken Spiro, "Exile," *Crash Course in Jewish History #38,* http://www.aish.com/jl/h/48945366.html.

5. M. E. Yapp, *The Making of the Modern Near East 1792–1923* (Harlow, England: Longman, 1987), 290.

6. Ricki Hollander, "Anti-Jewish Violence in Pre-State Palestine/1929 Massacres," Committee for Accuracy in Middle East Reporting in America, August 23, 2009, http://www.camera.org/index.asp?x_context=55&x_article=1691.

7. Yosef Kats, *Partner to Petition: The Jewish Agency's Partition Plan in the Mandate Era* (London: Routledge, 1998), ch. 4.

8. Paul Johnson, "Part Seven: Zion, The War of Israel's Independence," *A History of the Jews* (New York: Harper & Row, 1987), 527.

9. Mitchell G. Bard, *The Complete Idiot's Guide to the Middle East Conflict*, 4th ed. (New York: Alpha Books, 2008), 177–178.

10. Mammad Salah al-Din, *Al-Misri,* April 12, 1954, quoted in "The Suez War of 1956," Jewish Virtual Library, http://www.jewishvirtual library.org/jsource/History/Suez_War.html.

11. Committee for Accuracy in Middle East Reporting in America, "This Is Peacemaking?" *Snapshots* (blog), February 27, 2007, http://blog .camera.org/archives/2007/02/this_is_peacemaking.html.

12. Committee for Accuracy in Middle East Reporting in America, "Precursors to War: Arab Threats against Israel," *The Six-Day War,* accessed August 23, 2012, http://www.sixdaywar.org/content/threats .asp.

13. Charles Krauthammer, "Prelude to the Six Days," *Washington Post*, May 18, 2007, A23.

14. George Otis Sr., *The Ghost of Hagar*, 2nd ed. (Van Nuys, Calif.: Time-Light Books, 1974), 31–33.

15. William B. Quandt, *Peace Process: American Diplomacy and the Arab-Israeli Conflict Since 1967*, 3rd ed. (Washington, D.C. and Los Angeles: Brookings Institution Press and the University of California Press, 2005), 104.

16. Mitchell Bard, "The Yom Kippur War," Jewish Virtual Library, http://www.jewishvirtuallibrary.org/jsource/History/73_War.html.

17. Gary Thoma, "The Return of the Jewish Church," *Christianity Today*, September 7, 1998.

Chapter 8: Bringing "Life from the Dead"

1. Ruth Tucker, *Not Ashamed: The Story of Jews for Jesus* (Colorado Springs: Multnomah, 1999), Kindle edition.

Chapter 9: Rabbi, What More Can I Do?

1. Rose Price, *A Rose From the Ashes: The Rose Price Story* (San Francisco: Purple Pomegranate Productions, a Division of Jews For Jesus, 2006), 81.

Chapter 10: A Step Further

1. John Gimbel, *Science, Technology, and Reparations: Exploitation and Plunder in Postwar Germany* (Palo Alto, Calif.: Stanford University Press, 1990).

2. Dennis Prager, "Those Who Curse the Jews and Those Who Bless Them," *Jewish World Review*, July 31, 2002, http://www.jewishworld review.com/0802/prager073102.asp.

3. Bill Koenig, *Eye to Eye: Facing the Consequences of Dividing Israel* (Springfield, Mo.: 21st Century Press, 2007), 163–171.

4. Jonathan Bernis, *Is Peace Possible? A Historical and Biblical Understanding of Current Events in the Middle East* (Phoenix: Jewish Voice Ministries International, 2011), 43–44.

5. Richard Esposito, et al., "Joplin Death Toll at 116 Making It Deadliest Tornado in Nearly Sixty Years," ABC News, May 23, 2011, abcnews .go.com/US/Joplin-tornado-death-toll-116-makes-deadliest-single/story ?id=13662193.

6. William Koenig, *Koenig's Eye View* (blog), *World Watch Daily*, January 13, 2012, www.watch.org.

7. Yechiel Eckstein, *What You Should Know About Jews and Judaism* (Nashville: W Publishing, 1984), 288.

8. Ibid.

9. Ibid.

Jonathan Bernis has worked on the forefront of world evangelism since 1984, taking the Good News of Israel's Messiah to the far reaches of the earth. He serves as president of Jewish Voice Ministries International (JVMI), where the mission is twofold: 1) to proclaim the Gospel to the Jew first and then to the nations (see Romans 1:16), and 2) to equip the Church to reach the Jewish people. JVMI educates Christians on the Hebraic roots of Christianity, the Church's responsibility to Israel, and how to share Messiah with the Jewish people.

Jonathan's weekly television program, "Jewish Voice with Jonathan Bernis," airs throughout the U.S., Canada, Europe, Africa and Asia. JVMI also proclaims the Good News through print media and large-scale international Festivals of Jewish Music & Dance in Eastern Europe, India and South and Central America, as well as humanitarian/medical outreaches to the Lost Tribes of the House of Israel—the poorest Jewish communities on earth located in places such as India and Africa.

A sought-after speaker, Jonathan also teaches at seminars and conferences worldwide. He is a passionate supporter of Israel and a prominent leader in the Messianic movement. He is the author of several books, including *A Rabbi Looks at Jesus of Nazareth*; *Is Peace Possible? Understanding the Current Middle East Crisis*; *Confessing the Hebrew Scriptures: Adonai—Jehova Rof•e•cha—"The Lord Your Healer"*; *How to Share Yeshua*; *A Hope and a Future*; *The Expanding Kingdom*; and *7 Keys to Unlock the Prophetic Mysteries of Israel*.

Jonathan and his wife, Elisangela, are the parents of two daughters, Liel and Hannah, and reside in Phoenix, Arizona.

All of history hangs on the answer to one question:
Who is Jesus of Nazareth?

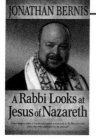

A Rabbi Looks at Jesus of Nazareth

Raised in a traditional Jewish family, international television host Jonathan Bernis was taught from a young age that "Jews don't—and can't!—believe in Jesus." Yet in his study of the Scriptures, including the Torah, he found overwhelming evidence that Jesus of Nazareth really is the Jewish Messiah. With warmth and transparency, Bernis shares his journey of discovering Jesus, how it changed his life and how he answers questions such as

- What do the prophets say about Jesus?
- How did Jewish Yeshua become Gentile Jesus?
- Is the New Testament anti-Semitic?
- Whatever happened to Judaism?

If you are a Jewish person seeking the truth about who Jesus really was and is, Bernis offers you loving evidence that counters common Jewish objections— and reveals a very different picture of Jesus than you may have been taught growing up.

If you are a Christian with Jewish friends, Bernis will equip you with the tools and knowledge to gently share your faith with them in an informed manner.

You will be challenged by what you read, but you may be even more surprised by what you discover.

A Rabbi Looks at Jesus of Nazareth by Jonathan Bernis

chosenbooks.com